For Katie

Congratulations

on your graduation

+ best wishes at College

+ with your volleyball

Uncle Bob

June, 2009

The Untold Story of
William G. Morgan
Inventor of Volleyball

Joel B. Dearing

WingSpan Press

Printed in the United States of America

Published by WingSpan Press, Livermore, CA
www.wingspanpress.com

The WingSpan name, logo and colophon are the trademarks of
WingSpan Publishing.

ISBN 978-1-59594-181-7

First Edition 2007

Library of Congress Control Number 2007932035

Contents

Acknowledgments

My initial research for this book was aided by three former students, Sean Byron, Chad O'Donnell, and Mark Straubel, who were most helpful. I am also grateful for the proofreading and language translation provided by Springfield College students Kait Kozak and Hitomaru Aoki. The Morgan family background was provided by the late Mary Quackenbush, along with Jack Deeringer, Henry "Hank" Schmidt, and John Gartner.

I would like to thank Mark Albiez, who serves as the executive director of the Lockport YMCA, and Lockport historian Richard Dickenson for their help. I also received great cooperation and assistance from the Niagara Historical Society and the Lockport, New York, Library staff.

I thoroughly enjoyed collaborating with the late Ed Crowe on his video project, "The William G. Morgan Story," and received valuable advice from him. Ed's photographer, Buc Williams, was also very helpful to me in providing photos for this book.

More recently, I have received support in my efforts to publish this book from Dr. Stephen Coulon, my department chair at Springfield College. Thank you Stephen for your encouragement. Thanks also to Peter Weis, archivist at the Northfield Mount Hermon School, for his time and helpful attention to detail in my search for specific information from the school records.

Over the years, I have also received assistance from many staff members from the Volleyball Hall of Fame and wish to thank them collectively for their help. Thanks also to the staff of the Babson Library at Springfield College and in particular Eleanor Corridan, Rachel Naismith, Gary Atwood, Andrea Taupier, and archivist Paige Roberts, who has been especially helpful to me in the final stages of my efforts.

Fran Hamel, Christine Nader, and Ray Long were able to point me in the right direction as I searched the Spalding

Company archives and in particular, was able to review original materials from the Spalding Athletic Library.

Professor Paul Thornton, from Springfield Technical Community College, provided some helpful advice in connecting me to WingSpan Press. Thank you Paul.

A very special thank you to Shannon Langone, my editor, who really was the impetus for getting this book to print.

David Collins from WingSpan Press provided encouragement and was the final piece of the puzzle in publishing this book. Margaret Hand from WingSpan Press was also most helpful in guiding me through all of the final revisions.

I do wish to thank my wife, Diane, and our children, Erin, Kevin, and Ryan, who always have been so very supportive of me, the work I do at Springfield College, and my career.

Dedication

In memory of Tom Hay, my Springfield College volleyball coach and a pioneer in the establishment of collegiate volleyball in the eastern United States, and to Sunday school teachers and Christian workers everywhere.

Introduction

Volleyball is a unique sport that combines power, speed, and finesse. It is a game that provides opportunities for athletes of every size to display their ferocious attacks or amazing quickness and diving saves. The Olympic Games features both six-person indoor teams and two-person sand court competitions. Volleyball is an international sport that continues to attract ever-expanding audiences who witness and enjoy the excitement, flair, and shifts of momentum, all aspects of the nature of the game.

And volleyball is, first and foremost, a game. A game played in all sorts of places. A game played by any number and mixture of people—boys and girls, men and women, old and young. It's all about putting the ball on the floor or the ground or the sand, or it's all about keeping the ball in the air. You have probably played the game and tried to do both. Spiking the ball to the ground or diving to keep it in the air—those are the moments when you feel the game.

Volleyball originated as a response, really, to a new game called basketball. William G. Morgan came under the influence of the inventor of basketball, James Naismith, while attending the YMCA Training School, now known as Springfield College, in Massachusetts. In just his first year on the job as a YMCA professional in Holyoke, Massachusetts, Morgan responded to the rough play exhibited by basketball participants by contemplating and creating an alternative sport. Morgan designed the game as a lunchtime activity for local businessmen, one that would require teamwork but would eliminate the fierce physical combat of basketball. This game would provide some exercise and entertainment but cut out the bloody noses and rugbylike scrums becoming all too common on the basketball court. Morgan's idea was to simply divide two teams with a net. Borrowing from tennis and badminton, Morgan improvised to allow participants the opportunity to play without contact from their opponents. The goal of the game was also simple: Put the ball on the floor of the opponent's court.

Much has been written about the history of Morgan's idea, but very little has been recorded about the man behind the game. His story is one that begs to be told, as it reveals his path to the birthplace of volleyball, a path of twists and turns and a few adventurous detours. Morgan proved to be an intelligent and well-educated man despite dropping out of school in his midteens. He was a bit of an explorer and risk-taker early in life, but somewhat wishy-washy and random too, especially after he left YMCA work after just a few short years in that career. As a youngster, he consistently expressed his desire to become an engineer but strayed from that path more than once, with mixed results.

I was initially motivated to tell this story because of my own connections to the sport of volleyball, to Springfield College, and to the Volleyball Hall of Fame. In anticipation of the centennial celebration of volleyball in 1995, I began to dig a little deeper into Morgan's life. Venturing to his hometown of Lockport, New York, meeting with his relatives, and discovering bits and pieces of his life story increased my interest in connecting the dots of people, places, and events that led to the development of a sport that is one of the most played in the world.

Morgan is a fellow alumni of Springfield College. My own involvement at the college for more than twenty years, and my understanding of the significant historical role of our college both in the development of physical education programs and professionals and in contributions to the world of sport, made me want to tell this story. A record of Morgan's life, the impact he had, and the impact the college had on him are important historically for Springfield College.[1] During his short time at the college, he was prepared for a brief yet wonderfully productive YMCA career that would yield a very popular and important sport.

Morgan left a most enjoyable legacy to the world. He attended schools founded by evangelists and pastors that were designed to prepare young men for Christian service. During his career, Morgan came face to face with businessmen in need of a lunchtime activity, and the concept he developed to "serve" them "serves" us still.

Both very notable and otherwise anonymous people played significant roles in the chain of events that led to Morgan being in a position to invent a sport, let alone a sport that would bring honor to him and his family long after his death. Most of us can relate to Morgan's experience when we look back at those who influenced our career paths. It only takes one or two people who strongly believe in our potential and are willing to go above and beyond in promoting that potential to others to make the difference in the professional lives we lead.

It is difficult to determine the actual influence and support of Morgan's own family, but it seems clear that his father was a successful boatbuilder, and it is easy to imagine that the creativity involved in that craft may have rubbed off on William and his own ability to pursue his imagination and ideas. It is more clear that behind the scenes William had a very faithful mother whose strong character impressed local folks in Lockport, and at least one local and rather obscure woman, a Sunday school teacher, took the extra step to promote William when he was at an early crossroads in his life.

Fortunately for every volleyball enthusiast, Morgan did step away from some of his initial life goals and found himself in the right place at the right time to design and introduce a sport that outlived him and exceeded any expectations he could have had the first time he strung a tennis net across the Holyoke YMCA gym.

1

The Morgans of Lockport, New York

George Henry Morgan was born in Pembrokeshire, Wales. His father, Enoch, was a butcher in the village of Pembroke Dock. His mother, Margaret Morgan, took care of George and his two brothers following the death of his father. George's older brother, William, took over the family business and cattle farm, while George and his younger brother, Alfred, completed seven years of apprenticeships, training as ship's carpenters.[1]

After finishing their apprenticeships, George and Alfred were able to make an arrangement to leave Wales and sail for America. They paid for this adventure by working on the ship and making repairs during their journey, and they took their onboard repair work very seriously since neither brother could swim.[2]

The Morgan brothers arrived in America in 1861, settling first in St. Louis and working for the government as boatbuilders. One of their friends, Thomas Nash, encouraged them to relocate to the Buffalo, New York, area. Shortly after arriving in Buffalo, George seriously injured his hand while working on the dry docks. In 1862, he moved to Lockport, New York, and established a dry dock and boatbuilding company with an associate, Mr. James Sutton.[3]

In 1816, the New York State Legislature finalized the decision to construct the Erie Canal. As plans for the exact location of the canal were developed and announced, large plots of land were purchased as investments. The village of Lockport grew quickly as the Erie Canal labor force moved in. In 1824, Lockport was organized as a town, and in October of 1825, the canal in Lockport was officially opened.[4]

Lockport thrived as work at the canal continued. Efforts to increase the original size of the canal from four feet deep and forty feet wide to seven feet deep and seventy feet wide were initiated in 1838, and the project was finally completed in 1860.

It was two years later that George H. Morgan arrived in this Erie Canal town. His brother Alfred followed him six years later, arriving in 1868. He joined George's company in 1878, and a year later he purchased Mr. Sutton's share of the business to become a partner in the Morgan Brothers Boat Building Company. The Morgan brothers' business occupied a prime location on the eastern side of Lockport on the wide water of the barge canal, and for many years their company thrived.

The December 8, 2006 *Lockport Union-Sun & Journal* described the Morgan boats as the best around. The following account details the specifics of their business.

> Their lower Market Street location gave them a commercial advantage in a region that thrived on the availability of water, power and access to easy transportation. The Morgan Brothers built canal boats, steam propellers and yachts, as well as a large number of boats and dredges that were ordered by the Canadian government. During the heyday of their business, the company employed upward to fifty men and purchased a large amount of machinery to ply their trade. The Morgan Brothers boat yard consisted of a woodworking building, a carpenter's paint shop, a canal boat building, a storage

building, three dry docks and an office. The average employment was thirty-five men. The Lockport boat builders used the latest saws and equipment of that time, which allowed for planks to be hewn from trees that would run the full length of canal boats. Once launched, a boat would be towed up the canal to Hall Iron Works for installation of steam boilers. Because of these steam boilers, Morgan boats were among the first boats that could be used on the Great Lakes as well as the Erie Canal.[5]

Soon after his arrival in Lockport, George had enrolled in a writing school to help him accommodate the injury he had sustained to his right hand. He grew fond of his teacher, Nancy Chatfield, who hailed from Northfield, Vermont. George and Nancy eventually married and had six children. William G. Morgan, their first son, was born on January 23, 1870.

2

Young Will — "Well Worth Polishing"

Young Will Morgan was larger than other boys his own age, and it appears that he fell behind in his studies to the point of being grouped with younger and smaller classmates. Uncomfortable with his size in comparison to other students, Will reports later in life that he "ran away from home at 14 to become a helper on a canal boat."[1] Will eventually received permission to leave school at the age of fifteen. He began to work on the canal boats and hoped his training would help prepare him to be qualified as an engineer. However, these early years of labor proved to be a challenge for his character.

George Morgan insisted that his children fend for themselves as early as they were able. Will traveled throughout the region as part of his work and along the way encountered many unsavory companions. Apparently, his own strong spiritual convictions, planted in him by a faithful mother, enabled him to stand tall in the face of worldly temptations.

Will began to approach a crossroads in his life as he realized that if he wanted to become an engineer he needed to further his education. He dreamed of pursuing an engineering course at Cornell University and determined that some preliminary studies at the Mount Hermon School would help him achieve this goal. Will had two friends who had recommended Mount Hermon, so at the age of twenty, he penned a letter to the headmaster of the Massachusetts boarding school. His letter of November 6, 1890, was addressed to Mr. Henry E. Sawyer.

> Dear Sir:
> I have been thinking quite seriously of fitting myself for a Mechanical Engineer and to make a success of my profession I am in need of an education. There has been two of my gentlemen friends attending school at Mount Hermon and they recommend it and advise me to take a term or two and more if possible. I understand the tuition is very reasonable and my means are limited so I thought I would try to procure admission. I would like to enter next February if possible or as soon as you can make a place.
> Yours truly, William G. Morgan[2]

Records kept at the Mount Hermon School indicate that Will's official application for admission, completed by his father, soon followed.

> 1. Full name of candidate for admission. *William G. Morgan*
> 2. Birthplace. *Lockport, NY*
> 3. Send a physician's certificate as to health, specifying any weakness.
> 4. Has candidate done anything toward self-support? *Steam Engineering*
> 5. What schools attended and how long? *Primary school, and Lockport Union School from the age of five to fifteen*
> 6. Amount of work done in the following studies giving rank if possible.
> Arithmetic. *As far as banking*
> Grammar and analysis. *Rudiments*
> Geography. *Through Common School Geography*

U.S. History. *None*

7. If higher branches have been studied, state amount of work done in each.

8. Any marked preferences in study, reading and occupation? *Mathematics. Works on machinery and mechanical improvements. Engineering.*

9. Has candidate shown an ambition to excel in anything? *He has*

10. Has he formed any purpose in life? *He has decided to qualify himself for a Mechanical Engineer.*

11. What prominent traits of character. *Nothing special*

12. Has he had any bad companions? *No*

13. Does he use tobacco? *No* Has he any bad habits? *No*

14. Any evidence of piety? *No*

15. Is he a member of any church? *He is*

16. In what religious belief educated? *Methodist*

17. Why do you wish to send him to this school? *To secure an education which will be of advantage to him in the business that he has chosen to follow*

18. Does the candidate himself wish to come here? *He does*

19. Full names and addresses of father, mother, guardian, or nearest friend. *Father, Geo H. Morgan Lockport, NY*

20. Are they in church membership? *Mother member of Methodist Church. Father not a member of any Church*

21. Their occupation and means? *Boat builder, means limited*

22. Who will be responsible for the pupil's support? *Father*

23. Send address of pastor and some businessman. *Robert Norton J. S. Helmer*[3]

There is much to learn from this completed application.

Will's father appeared to support Will's desire to attend Mount Hermon. Will had made it clear to his father that he wanted to pursue engineering, and Will saw applying to Mount Hermon as a first step in that process. While Will gained the backing of his father, his application was by no means a sure thing. Mount Hermon was established by evangelist D. L. Moody and generally accepted only underprivileged boys, and most of these students did not stay on through graduation. Will gained critically important support from a local Sunday school teacher, Mrs. J. S. Helmer, who wrote an initial letter of recommendation on November 10, 1890, addressed to the principal of the Mount Hermon School. This letter gives helpful insight into Will's upbringing and in particular some idea of his mother's impact on his development and character. Mrs. Helmer wrote,

> With this mail there goes an application of Will G. Morgan's and I wish to write in regard to him, and the reasons why his case should be considered. He is, as you will see from date given, twenty years old; he is large—over six feet in height. From a child he was always large—larger than those of his own age and getting behind in his studies he became ashamed to sit with small boys in class—became unwilling to go to school and at his age of fifteen was permitted to drop out and go to work. Having always liked engineering—advanced to be ready for papers as a regularly qualified engineer. Now he begins to feel his lack of education. He has come to me as a friend and S. Sch. Teacher wishing he might go to Mt. Hermon and then when ready—enter Cornell University Engineering Course. This is the crisis of his life—between being a common or a superior man.
>
> Now as to why there is reason to hope much for him. First, he is a true, tested Christian. He has worked on the Canal, Hudson River, and been about New York, known among bad

companions and came out safe. Has even tried to distribute tracts, etc.

His father is an upright business man of moderate means. With a large family—he expects them to care for themselves as soon as able. Will has earned the money with which to go to Mt. Hermon and purposes to work his way through, although his father will help, if it becomes necessary.

His mother is a remarkable woman. A devout Christian, a "main stay" in her Church; calm, quiet, dignified in her bearing, she purchases ably and shows great executive ability earnestly and most devoutly does she work and pray for the good of young people of East Lockport. I say much of her because I think such a mother's son has power in him. He is an unpolished stone which I believe you have the privilege of fitting to accomplish his Master's bidding—I therefore beg you to prayerfully consider his application. Will is in the same class that Geo. Turner and John Tildsley came from. And I refer you to Geo. Turner who graduated last year as to Will's ability. Trusting as soon as possible Will may be admitted.

Respectfully, L. F. Helmer (Mrs. J. S.)[4]

A local pastor, R. Norton, wrote to Mr. W. F. Cutter in support of Will, stating, "He is very thoughtful and interested in spiritual things. He is very reliable and has much symmetry of character."[5] These comments may have provided significant commentary for Will, particularly in light of this statement on Mt. Hermon's application for admission: "Among the indispensable conditions of admission are a sound mind and a sound body."[6] Pastor Norton continued in his recommendation by describing Will's mother as "a woman of high qualities."[7]

These letters appear to have provided powerful support intended to effectively persuade the Mt. Hermon administrators to admit Will. A second letter from Mrs. Helmer written on December 31, 1890, shows that Will was not immediately accepted. Will's future and what would become his remarkable place in history as the inventor of volleyball may never have come to pass had it not been for Mrs. Helmer's persistent and convincing advocacy for his candidacy. It's difficult to imagine that Will did not return to Mrs. Helmer, perhaps numerous times, to ask her for advice in the process of gaining admission to Mount Hermon. It is just as likely, given the records found of her written recommendation letters, that Mrs. Helmer may have remained in contact with Will or his mother while waiting to hear the good news of his acceptance. Speculation aside, it's clear that this Sunday school teacher went above and beyond her call by writing a follow-up letter. The depth of her own conviction is evident as she expresses her grave concern for this worthy young man and pleads for consideration on his behalf. Her writing style is quite entertaining, as she respectfully brings attention to her cause while acknowledging the potential sea of applicants that Will was surely competing with for admission. Mrs. Helmer wrote the following letter addressed to the principal of Mount Hermon.

> Pardon my troubling you again, but I wish to remind you of William G. Morgan's application sent in two or three months ago. I wrote you at length then, but fear in the multitude of such letters, mine is quite buried. I simply write to ask attention to it, as his call is critical. If Will is not accepted now, for term beginning in Feb., there is great reason to fear he will never go to school again. Not from his wish, but from circumstances. Both George Turner and John Tildsley who know him, say he is just such as they want there. A thoroughly established Christian, inheriting from his mother superior qualities of mind and heart, he is well worth

polishing for his Master's use. I beg your
attention to his application.
Respectfully, Mrs. J. S. Helmer[8]

There is a lesson here about the power of a reference
letter and the potential influence of such strong support.
Additionally, Mrs. Morgan and many parents may never
realize the admiration that others have for the job they do in
modeling, guiding, and directing their children through all the
phases of childhood and adolescence. Mrs. Morgan, at least in
the estimation of her friend, had been a faithful and influential
parent, and her son was destined for success.

Within a week of this letter, Will was notified of his
acceptance to Mount Hermon, perhaps never to know the
impact of the Sunday school teacher he had confided in or the
personal and positive nature and contents of her letters. George
H. Morgan wrote a letter of confirmation to Mr. Henry Cutter
on January 6, 1891. This letter was written on the stationery of
the Morgan Brothers Boat Building Company. Events moved
swiftly once Will was accepted, and Mr. Morgan's letter
provides some insight into the final arrangements.

Dear Sir: Yours of Jan. 3rd and contents noted,
and in reply would say we will endeavor to meet
the requirements mentioned as our son as well
as ourselves are quite anxious to get started in
this matter of an education. Therefore you may
consider this an acceptance of the privilege of
his becoming a student at your institution.
Yours truly, Geo H. Morgan

P.S. Since writing the above I find that it is not
possible for William to get to Mount Hermon
from this place in one day, therefore if it is
essential for him to be there before the school
opens he can leave here on the Friday previous
and arrive at your place on Saturday Jan. 31 or

on Tuesday Feb. 3. Please advise what you think
best.

GHM[9]

Will had come to the crossroads of his young life and now
prepared to step ahead on a path that he seemed convinced
would lead him to Cornell University. He could not have
known then how this path would continue to veer in the years
ahead. Will headed off to Massachusetts, leaving behind the
canal and his family, unaware of the dots still to be connected
that would lead him to a completely unforeseen destiny.

3

Mount Hermon School — "Lazy Boys Are Not Desired"

Dwight Lyman (D. L.) Moody was born in 1837 in Northfield, Massachusetts. Moody was a great evangelist who became known for his commitment to Christian education. He established the Northfield School for Girls in 1879 and the Mount Hermon School for Boys in 1881. Moody envisioned schools that promoted a well-rounded education, with biblical training as the foundation of the experience for the students. The development of both of these schools led to the initiation of summer Bible conferences aimed at adults and college students. By 1886, the summer conference program had expanded to include a month-long session for college students. The result of this conference included a pledge from one hundred participants to enter a foreign missionary service at the completion of their education. By the following year, more than two thousand students became part of what would become the Student Volunteer Movement.[1]

The first person to assist D. L. Moody in the establishment of the Mount Hermon School was Hiram Camp. His gift of $25,000 enabled Mr. Moody to purchase a piece of land bordering 175 acres that he already had in his possession. Mr. Camp suggested the name Mount Hermon from a passage of

Scripture found in Psalms 133:3:[2] "As the dew of Hermon, and as the dew that descended upon the mountains of Zion: for there the Lord commanded the blessing, even life for evermore." This verse provided the foundation for the development of a school for boys.

From the outset, boys enrolled at Mount Hermon adhered to a daily routine of daily chapel, silent time for devotions, physical activity and recreation, and manual labor in addition to their academic studies. Initially, the school served boys ages eight to twelve, but within a few years, the minimum age for acceptance was set at sixteen.[3] Ten years after the vision of D. L. Moody became a reality, William G. Morgan enrolled.

The 1891–92 Mount Hermon catalog issued this warning to those submitting applications for admission: "Lazy boys are not desired."[4] Indeed, the school was designed for young men who had conceived a serious purpose in life, for those, like Will, earnest in their desire to receive an education, and for those longing to know more of the Bible. The school was for young men with sound bodies, good minds, and high aims. Mrs. J. S. Helmer and others felt that Will fit this description.

Will and his classmates worked two to three hours a day under the direction of a local farmer. Will also worked in the school laundry to help pay for his tuition. He and his classmates developed positive work habits in this environment, and their service contributed to the operation of the school.

Students attended classes from 7:45 a.m. to 12:15. In addition to his scheduled classes and evening study hours, Will took part in the music program at Mount Hermon. His academic records indicate his involvement in the chorus and elocution, a select quartet. The pianist for these young men, Mary King Caldwell, would eventually become Will's wife. As part of this singing quartet, Will traveled to surrounding churches with D. L. Moody, singing on evangelistic tours.[5]

Students were encouraged by the officials at Mount Hermon to be gentlemen at all times. They were expected to be courteous, prompt, and faithful to all duties. They were even admonished by their classmates to strongly consider their behavior in chapel. In an editorial found in the school paper, *The Hermonite,* students were asked to reconsider the temptation of a quick escape from daily services. An excerpt from one edition of the paper reads, "Hoe out your row is the terse advice of a College exchange in commenting on the practice of jumping up before the last notes of a closing hymn have died away. We have a few students here who seem to consider the last three words of the hymn at devotions as the Ready! Set! Go! of the starter. It has been estimated that they gain three minutes a year by this practice. But they do it at the expense of civility to their neighbors, if not of reverence to God."[6] Will's reverence to God must have been apparent to his peers, as he was elected chaplain by his class.[7]

Will found himself in a community of faculty, administrators, and students concerned with self-discipline and attitude. He decided to add one more school activity to challenge and develop those characteristics even more by using his physical abilities. His size and strength, once a source of discomfort, were now a potential advantage as he engaged in the pursuit of a sporting activity, most notably as a fine center on the school's football team.

Mount Hermon lost their 1891 season opening match against Greenfield by a score of 4 to 6 on November 14. On November 17, Will and his teammates rebounded with a shutout victory (30–0) over Battleboro (Vermont) High School. They completed their season with an 80 to 0 thrashing over Cushing in a game played at Crystal Lake.[8]

While modern-day American football teams may often focus on quarterbacks, running backs, and linebackers as the keys to victory, the late-nineteenth-century teams prized a powerful center who could anchor the offense and help the team push down the field. Will's impressive stature and powerful play were on display as his Mount Hermon team opened their 1892 campaign on October 13, but it was the next game on the schedule that would contribute to a permanent departure from his plan of heading to Cornell University.

4

Naismith — The Recruiter

On October 21, 1892, William G. Morgan suited up for another football game. The opponent for the Mount Hermon team on this day was the Springfield YMCA Training School. The Training School, incorporated in 1885 as the School for Christian Workers, was led by one of their faculty members— player/coach James Naismith. Naismith's charges, dubbed "the Stubby Christians,"[1] were already gaining a reputation as a tough opponent on the football field. The school's mission was to train young men to go into YMCA work, and the heavy regimen of physical activity courses required of those enrolled there led some to refer to the Springfield, Massachusetts, institution as the "straining" school.[2]

The Springfield football program was established in 1890, when Amos Alonzo Stagg arrived on campus. Stagg had been captain and top player at Yale for both the baseball and football teams and had helped Yale on the field to victories over longtime rivals Princeton and Harvard. "Stagg's eleven" made a name for themselves quickly with a win over Amherst in their first campaign and a remarkable 10 to 16 loss to Yale in a special event held in Madison Square Garden.[3] James Naismith was on that squad and took over as player/coach by the fall of 1892.

Naismith was just gaining notoriety for the invention of a new game called basket ball, but he was also a familiar figure on the Mount Hermon campus, as he and notable YMCA Training School faculty, including Luther Halsey Gulick, made regularly scheduled visits to the campus to lead physical activity and YMCA classes.

Naismith attended the YMCA Training School and was listed as an instructor in the school's 1892–93 catalog. He taught several courses, including Study of the Bible by Books, Outline Study of Man, Ethics, and Methods of Christian Work for Seniors. He worked for Dr. Gulick, who served as the school's superintendent of the Physical Department, and also worked alongside Dr. A. T. Halsted, who would later become a significant person in Morgan's invention of the game of volleyball. Dr. Halsted was in charge of the department's correspondence course and also taught Physical Examinations and Gymnastics Therapeutics.[4]

The Stubby Christians prevailed in this hard-fought contest by a score of 16 to 8. It appears likely that Will Morgan's play so impressed the visiting coach that Dr. Naismith may have invited him to consider continuing his education in Springfield and joining his team. Naismith surely had an eye for talent, and his recruiting efforts proved to be influential. Records at Mount Hermon indicate that Morgan interrupted his course of study by withdrawing from the school on October 25, 1892[5] — just four days after meeting Naismith's team on the field. The November 12, 1892, edition of *The Hermonite* confirms Morgan's departure—"The fates indeed seemed combined against the football team this year. Morgan was induced to leave and attend The Training School, Springfield, where he is playing center."[6]

The October 1892 International Association Training School Notes, a monthly bulletin, lists William G. Morgan as a junior and the "center" on the football team. James Naismith is listed as the fullback. It is noted that "Mr. Naismith has not only had the responsibility of teaching the game to all the students, but is the captain of the first team as well, and has done fine work".[7]

Additional insight into Morgan's experience at the Training School is provided in the October 1892 Training School Notes through the following article.

Football of 1892

Football is doubtless the most popular game in this country today. All the best principal colleges have teams, and a noted feature is that many of the best men in college are on those teams. It is a game which attracts the strong, because a man must be muscular to play it. It attracts the man who excels in mental strength, because it is such an exceedingly scientific game. It attracts the courageous man, because it demands the quality in its players. It attracts the Christian man, because it requires self-control and enables him to show his ability to enter into sports, play a clean game, and at the same time do better work than the man who loses his temper and lays aside those qualities which go to make up a man.

There are many other reasons, but these are sufficient to warrant our school in devoting a fraction of time to the instruction of those who are to be leaders of young men in their athletic exercise, as well as in other things, in this popular and manly game. A part of this present fall term has been spent in teaching every man to play the game, and daily we have at least three full teams on the ground at work. These teams play against each other very often, and the theory becomes practice. Each man is played in all the different positions so he may know every man's part in each play, and he also takes his turn in coaching. Of course, when a game is played each man has the position for which he is specially qualified, but the training of each man to become a teacher is kept constantly in mind.[8]

This philosophical summary of the purpose of the football program and Morgan's experiences as a member of the team help to provide a view of organized athletics during this period of time. This description also offers insight into the reputation of Springfield College as a coaching factory.

Morgan is listed as a junior at the International YMCA Training School for the 1892–93 academic year and is pictured with the Training School's 1893 football team along with Coach Naismith. The front page of the December 28, 1942, edition of the *Lockport Union-Sun & Journal* contains a summary of the Morgan years of football at the Training School: "In those days, the name of Springfield was sufficient to strike terror to the hearts of the best football squads in the East. In the days when football featured the flying wedge and other bone-crushing maneuvers, Springfield defeated the best of the University teams Harvard, Yale, Princeton and others."[9]

Morgan had no way of knowing the eventual significance of the recruiting prowess of James Naismith. This innovative sports leader would soon have reason to be quite proud of this particular pupil.

5

Springfield Days

Springfield College, known first as the School for Christian Workers, was opened on January 5, 1885. The First Statement of what would become the annual college catalog outlined the school's foundational mission.

> There has been developed a pressing and growing need for men to enter the various fields of Christian Work now open to laymen. The demand is especially pressing for men fitted to be secretaries of Young Men's Christian Associations, Superintendents of Sunday Schools, and helpers of pastors in mission work and in the general work of the Church. Experience and testimony have shown that there are many young men who would gladly enter these fields, and who would be abundantly successful, had they proper training.[1]

The School for Christian Workers was opened to "help meet this demand, and to train these men."[2]

The school's Second Statement included testimonials from many men with excellent reputations and various backgrounds in Christian service. Five such testimonials received were from men listed as lecturers for the opening year of the school. The endorsements from these men all pointed out the need for just such a school.

D. L. Moody, a noted evangelist and a strong educational proponent, wrote to Reverend David Allen Reed, founder of the School for Christian Workers. His letter indicates his support for Reed's vision.

> My dear friends—The School for Christian Workers will meet a great need. Many city pastors have asked me to find laymen for them who would be skilled helpers in the Sunday School and mission work; but I could not do it for there was no school to train them. The call for such men is greater today than ever. Then the Young Men's Christian Association, trained as you propose, would have more power and win more souls. We want more laymen who know the Word of God, and how to use it, trained for practical work and able to lead. I will do what I can to help you. May God bless the enterprise. Yours truly, D. L. Moody.[3]

First-year instructor M. B. Riddle of the Hartford Theological Seminary identified this new School for Christian Workers as an experiment that deserved a trial in a letter that was also included in the school's second catalog.

> December 24, 1894
> Dear Sir—The school you propose to open will meet a growing want in the sphere of Christian activity. Because I am a pronounced advocate of thorough preparation for the Christian ministry, I am also an advocate of proper preparation for all duty which requires knowledge and skill. The pastors, especially in our large cities, need helpers, trained men. How can they get them

if there is no special effort made to provide them?

As you are well aware, you are trying an experiment; but it deserves a trial, and so far as I know your plans deserve success. You may rely upon me to do what I can to help you to make it a success, and to use every opportunity to commend it to the favorable attention of others. Give my very best wishes to your associates, and believe me, Yours truly, M. B. Riddle.[4]

Evangelist S. M. Sayford of Newton, Massachusetts, wrote to Reverend Reed to indicate that positions were readily available for trained Christian workers at the present time.

My dear brother:—Your letter with reference to The School for Christian Workers is duly received. You shall have hearty cooperation so far as my work will allow. Such a school, rightly conducted, must supply a need long since recognized by many engaged in special phases of Christian work. I could employ or secure the employment of several men in evangelistic work today, if I could select from men specially designed for such work.

The rapidly enlarging field of the Young Men's Christian Association makes a demand for trained secretaries which your contemplated school will meet in part, and I see no reason why it should not contribute very largely in supplying. Then, too, in my judgment, the Sunday Schools at no distant day will need men whose whole time shall be given to the office of superintendent. Your project is not only timely, but I believe, God-Given. May his richest blessing attend every effort made in this direction. Yours truly, S.M. Sayford.[5]

The Reverend G. F. Pentecost of Brooklyn, New York, agreed with Sayford's view that full-time Sunday school superintendents would be highly sought after in the not too distant future. He also pointed out the gap in the training currently offered by seminaries and the type of training this school could provide for effective lay leadership.

> My dear Sir: I need not tell you how heartily you have my sympathy in the new work you are inaugurating. In my view, it is a work greatly needed, not in the least interfering with the best work our seminaries are doing, and filling a gap for which they make no provision.
>
> What a boon your School will be to the scores, and I believe, hundreds of young men, and what a boon those same hundreds of young men will be to the Church, and to the work of the Lord in general! The great need for our Young Men's Christian Association is more efficient secretaries—men who know how to teach, as well as plan work. And the time is coming, in my judgment, when our larger Sunday Schools will need superintendents who will give their whole time to that work as a pastor does to his parish. But they must be trained men. I might fill sheets in pointing out fields for such workers as I hope you will train for Christ. Yours fraternally, Geo. F. Pentecost.[6]

One last statement came from the secretary of the American Home Missionary Society, Walter M. Barrows. He not only endorsed the concept of the school because many vacancies for lay work currently existed in Churches, but also went on to predict that this school would be the predecessor of other similar training grounds.

> New York, December 20, 1884
> Dear Brother:—While at Northampton last

Sunday I heard of the new school that you are soon to open for the purpose of training laymen for Christian work. It struck me at once as an excellent plan, the more I think of it the more favorably I am impressed with the importance of the work you are about to inaugurate. Our Churches are beginning to wake up to the need of utilizing the lay element, if the kingdom of Christ is to be carried forward. Already there are numerous openings for lay work, more openings than there are persons qualified to enter them. Such a school as you contemplate will meet a felt want in training such workers, and in fitting them for their various spheres of usefulness. For the purpose, then, for which it is intended, I think highly of your enterprise, and I trust that your example will be contagious, and that similar schools will be started in different parts of the land. Very cordially yours, Walter M. Barrows.[7]

Initially founded as the School for Christian Workers, the school is described by these men as an enterprise, a project, and an experiment that could potentially meet the need for the training of young men. Needs were evident in both the churches and in the ever-expanding YMCAs. It is interesting to note the initial mission of the YMCA, which was founded by Sir George Williams in London. At the time he established this new association for men in 1844, his desire was to respond to the hardships of the workingmen that he observed. His initial organization was designed to positively impact men socially, educationally, and religiously. It was much later that the physical activity component was added as YMCAs began to include gymnasiums in their development of facilities.[8]

The apparent cultural and community issues identified by early supporters of the School for Christian Workers provide strong clues as to why the school's name was changed to the YMCA Training School. The need for "trained" men was referred to repeatedly in the correspondence from Moody and the others. Those same letters also help to clarify the roles and duties of YMCA secretaries as men who were administrators and teachers.

The letters offered by Pentecost and Barrows predicted that similar schools would begin opening in other parts of the country, and their assertions were rapidly confirmed, as D. L. Moody announced in 1886 his plans to establish the Moody Bible Institute—a school that would train Christian workers.[9] In the summer of 1887, two years before Moody's school opened, he spoke to a group of Northfield students about this topic.

> Some of you may think I oppose theological seminaries. I want to say I believe we want thoroughly trained men. I don't think we have enough trained men. At the same time, we want some men to stand between the laity and the ministers. I don't know what you would call them—gap men. We want men to stand in the gap. There is such a thing as educating a man away from the rank and file. There is a class of men, I believe, that have got to be raised up to do what we used to call in the war bushwhacking. We want irregulars—men that will go out and do work that the educated ministers can't do: get in among the people, and identify themselves with the people.[10]

Moody and the others, sending letters from Boston, St. Louis, New York City, and Philadelphia, reassured Revered Reed. It appears there was a resounding agreement that his school would indeed meet a need and that men would be prepared to fill the gap.

By the fall of 1892, when William G. Morgan arrived at the Springfield campus, the school had for the last year officially been called the International YMCA Training School. The symbol of the school was the inverted equilateral triangle designed by Luther Gulick. The left and right sides of the triangle were adorned with the words *mind* and *body*, upholding and balancing the top side of the triangle labeled with the word *spirit*.[11] The triangle included a piece of scripture, Ephesians 4:13: "Till we all come in the unity of the faith, and of the knowledge of the son of God, unto a perfect man, unto the measure of the stature of the fullness of Christ."

Young Will, the son of a highly regarded Christian mother, had moved through Mount Hermon School and now found himself in Springfield, Massachusetts. He clearly had strayed from the path of pursuing a career in mechanical engineering. The education he would now encounter would be grounded in the desire of his new faculty to educate the whole person—in spirit, mind, and body.

Morgan's own life up to this point had exhibited some balance in these three areas. His spiritual growth had been observed and confirmed by Pastor Norton back in Lockport. He was a strong, active young man. He had achieved success in his physical pursuits, most notably as a football player. He had survived some educational obstacles as a young boy but had rebounded in time to reestablish his education as a priority. His professional calling may have been unclear to him as he entered the International YMCA Training School, but his commitment to academics was obvious.

Morgan was one of thirty juniors listed in the school's catalog for 1892–93 in the Physical Department. His classmates represented eleven states and several countries, including Ireland, Canada, and Scotland. The school's reputation had quickly grown in just seven years, and the curriculum was divided into three areas: General Course, Secretarial Department, and Physical Department.[12]

Morgan entered the Physical Department guided by the motto *E Tribus Unum*—From Three, One. The objective of the department was to train young men for the special duties of physical directors. According to the Training School's eighth catalogue, three specific principles formed the foundation of this department.

1. Unity. Man is a unit: body, mind and soul

forming one complete whole, neither complete without the others.

2. Law of Symmetry. The best results can be secured only when man as a whole is symmetrically developed, not merely each nature with reference to itself, but each nature in relation to others.

3. Function makes structure. The doing of a thing tends to increase the ability to do that thing. Thus, doing all-around exercises, those which demand symmetrical bodies tends to produce symmetry.

William's daily schedule included a full morning of department requirements.

8:00 — Systematic Bible Truth (3 hours/week) Abridged Secretarial Department Work (2 hours/week)
9:00 — Department Theory
10:00 — Daily Prayers/Activity
11:00 — Exercise

The school year lasted for forty weeks, and the students in the Physical Department received these estimates for their yearly expenses:

Table board	$100–$150
Furnished room with light and heat	$40–$55
Tuition	$50
Gymnasium suits	$15–$40
Washing	$12–$20
Text and note books	$20–$35
Conventions	$15–$18
Membership in local association	$2
Total	$254–$370[13]

William's Training School years were significant beyond his education and preparation for a YMCA career. During his time there, he married Mary King Caldwell on October 7, 1893. Mary was born in Northfield, Vermont, and first met her future husband when she served as the pianist for his Mount Hermon quartet. The Morgans stayed in Springfield until William's graduation in 1894.

Was William fully committed to a YMCA career at this time? Had he completely abandoned the pursuit of an engineering career? The answer to these questions may be apparent in the insights shared by others observing William during his time at the Training School. William graduated from a curriculum clearly intended to prepare him as a YMCA director, but the 1894 Training School Yearbook outlines the vision his classmates had for his future. The Class Prophesy, projected ten years ahead to July 1, 1904, predicted something other than a YMCA career for William.

> It was with a great degree of pleasure that I boarded one of the finest steamers of the world for the purpose of crossing the ocean to see some of our worthies who had voluntarily separated themselves from civilization. But my pleasure on this voyage was not confined to expectations of friendly greetings and brotherly hospitality upon reaching the shores of Europe. I had been invited to bunk with the engineer. That I considered a great privilege, for only those who were intimate with the controller of the power that drove the vessel through the restless waves, could gain admission to his sacred precincts. I remember how faithful Billy Morgan had been in small things, especially to that little moustache, so I was not surprised to find him entrusted with greater things, for it was he who was engineer.[14]

The author of this prophesy gives another little glimpse into Morgan's personality. Morgan was most likely known as Billy to his buddies and must have been a pretty regular guy, not averse to a little good-natured ribbing. At the same time, there could be a subtle message of admiration in the text with an obvious reference to Luke 16:10: "He that is faithful in that which is least is faithful also in much." In any case, it was no secret to his classmates that engineering was still on Morgan's mind even as he and his classmates left the Springfield campus.

Morgan's preparation at the Training School allowed him to enter YMCA work immediately, and he took his first position with the Auburn, Maine, YMCA.[15] Shortly after leaving Springfield, the Morgans celebrated the arrival of their first child. Lillian Morgan was born on June 30, 1894. By 1895, William had returned to Western Massachusetts to work at the Holyoke YMCA. On August 29 of that year, the Morgans were blessed with their first son, George.

6

Invention and Exhibition: From Mintonette to Volley Ball

In addition to balancing his new profession in YMCA work and his responsibilities as a father and a husband, William began to look for an innovative new game for the local businessmen to play. His mentor, James Naismith, had been successful in launching basketball, yet William and others were finding this game a bit too rough and rowdy for the group of local men who visited the Holyoke YMCA. He saw a need for a new, less strenuous recreational activity.

Morgan spent some time hitting a basketball back and forth with Holyoke fire chief John Lynch. They discovered that the ball was too heavy to keep in the air—the activity began to hurt their wrists. Morgan decided to try the same activity with the bladder of the ball, and he found this lighter ball much more comfortable to play with.[1]

He decided to approach a local company, A. G. Spalding and Brothers of Chicopee, Massachusetts, to request their help in designing a new ball. He came up with specifications for the circumference and weight of the ball and waited for delivery of the product. Initially, Spalding used a very soft calfskin material as a covering for the ball but found it wasn't durable and didn't wear well. The next prototype had a leather covering, similar to what the company was using on the basketball, and Morgan approved.

He introduced the concept of his new game in 1895. He stretched an old tennis net across the gymnasium; the net divided the playing surface, separated the teams on the court, and prevented body contact between opposing players. He established the height of the net at approximately six feet six inches to bring it above the average height of the men who came to his YMCA.[2] Morgan then divided the participants into two teams and instructed them to bat the ball back and forth to their teammates and across the net. After this introduction, Morgan continually experimented with the development of rules and strategies to be used during play. He referred to his game as "mintonette."

Later in life, Morgan recounted the initial design of his game and stated that the time, he "had no knowledge of any game similar to volleyball to aid him".[3]

Of interest is the arrival to America in 1895 of a game called "minton." This game was developed in India and was played outdoors on a forty by eighty foot surface. The game was adapted from lawn tennis, with teams of five players using ten ounce racquets to volley a six and one-half inch ball made of sheep's wool over a net that was 6 feet, 6 inches from the ground. Dr. Luther Gulick was one of the authors of a booklet published in 1896 that included the following description of this game, along with the rules.

> One of the oldest games of England—Badminton—has been totally changed by certain Englishmen, in India, through the introduction of a worsted ball in place of the shuttlecock which was formerly used. The game was brought to this country last year by Mr. David McConaughy, Jr. It possesses manifest advantages and opportunities in certain directions over other games, and notably over the one it is most like, viz: lawn-tennis.
> Some of the advantages are as follows: *First*, the

court does not need to be as carefully prepared. Any field that is smooth enough to run around on without danger of turning the ankles, is perfectly adapted to the purpose; a slight grade one way or the other does not materially alter the game.

Second, the cost of preparing the ground and keeping it in shape is almost nothing. The net being made of wire does not deteriorate, and does not need adjusting from time to time. The bats are far cheaper than tennis rackets of equal grade, and the balls are virtually indestructible.

Third, ten players in place of four are engaged at once. Thus the element of sociability is far more prominent than in lawn-tennis and more individuals exercise on the same space of ground, the size of the court being approximately the same as that for lawn-tennis.

Fourth, lawn-tennis is adapted for both men and women, and yet there are very few women who can play as well as passable players among the men, partly because it requires strength to handle the ball at the speed at which modern tennis is played. The Minton bat, however, is so light—only ten ounces—and the ball is so light—one half ounce—that the element of strength is almost entirely eliminated, so that the game is as available for women as for men, and teams made up partly of men and partly of women are not as lop-sided as such teams in almost all other games. There is no position, whether forward, center or back, that cannot be well played by women.

Fifth, the game is more interesting to the average spectator than lawn-tennis. The ball is in the air where it can be seen all the time; the playing fast; the rallies long, the ball sometimes being sent over the net twenty times before being driven to the ground. *Sixth*, the game is easy to learn, and commences to be thoroughly enjoyable after half an hour or so of practice. It has been decided to call the game Minton in place of badminton, as the changing of this implement, the ball, so changes the character of the game itself, and because Minton indicates both the similarity to and dissimilarity from the parent game, Badminton.[4]

The description of this game, including teams of players on a net that was 6 feet, 6 inches from the ground, has characteristics not unlike Morgan's original game of mintonette. Minton is described as a game that features teamwork and rallies, and an activity that grabs the interest of spectators, captured by the suspense of when the ball will hit the ground. Gulick and his coauthor, W. E. Allen, provide a diagram of the court and player positions (right back, left back, center, right forward, and left forward) and then continue on to describe the commencement of play. The authors summarize the game as follows:

There is a great deal of team play. In receiving all the team should go into the court, then get quickly into their places as soon as the serve is made and returned. If this is strictly adhered to, the ground will be well covered and the opponents will be puzzled as to where to place the ball. If a man hits the ball, but fails to send it over, other members of his team may hit it, provided no one man hits it twice, and excepting the service stroke.[5]

Not unlike the history of many modern games, it is not unusual for speculation about the original history and roots of a sport to appear in the form of theories advanced to raise questions, and offer alternative explanations. The game of minton needs to be looked at closely, considering the timing of its creation and presence in different parts of the world, including the United States.

In his book *Volleyball Its Origin and Development*, Japanese author Yutaka Mizutani proposes the theory that mintonette was in fact derived with the suffix "ette" added to the name of the Indian game of Minton. Mizutani suggests that "ette" can be translated to mean "similar to" or "like" so that Morgan's mintonette was a new game, played indoors, that was similar to the outdoor game of minton. He also offers strong opposition to any historical reference identifying "minonette" (sic) as the first name of volleyball.[6]

It does seem reasonable to consider the possibility that Morgan's intention may have been to credit aspects of the outdoor game minton that also were evident as characteristics of his indoor game, played without a racket. It's also possible that Morgan's use of the word "minton" in the naming of his new game was from his own adaptations of badminton. Whatever the true story behind the naming of this new game being played indoors at the Holyoke, MA, YMCA, those who were trying out this new activity were captured by its nature, and the game quickly grew in popularity.

Morgan was impressed by the YMCA members' enthusiastic reception, and he noted that "the staid businessmen used to forget themselves and jump right into the sport, so it filled the bill."[7]

It wasn't long before Dr. Luther Gulick, head of the Physical Department at the Springfield YMCA Training School, heard about this new game developed by a recent alumni. He invited Morgan to present mintonette to the participants of the Physical Director's Conference to take place on July 7, 1896.

William Morgan needed to prepare teams to participate in the first public exhibition of his new game, so he contacted the Holyoke mayor, J. J. Curran, and the local fire chief, John Lynch, designating them as the captains of two five-man mintonette squads.[8] He arranged for the teams, comprising local businessmen, to travel from Holyoke by trolley to the

Springfield YMCA Training School, where he would showcase his new game.

Morgan had also initiated the development of a few rules to govern the game, which were published for the first time a year later. The Holyoke businessmen demonstrated mintonette using Morgan's first set of rules, which essentially called for the ball to be put in play with a service and "volleyed" back and forth across the net by the teams. The ball could not be caught or held. To avoid this infraction, a player could use an air dribble by batting the ball to themselves, but only when they were behind a line on their side of the court located four feet from the net.

One of Morgan's former professors, A. T. Halsted, was in attendance on that July day in 1896 and made some observations regarding the nature of this new game. Noticing the continuous volleying of the ball between teammates and across the net to the opponents, Halsted suggested that a more appropriate name for this game would be "volley ball." Morgan quickly agreed to this suggestion.[9] While the game of volleyball was indeed born in Holyoke, the name of what would become a worldwide sport was established at the birthplace of basketball, a small school later to be known as Springfield College.

One can imagine Morgan's sense of pride on this occasion as he looked around the new gymnasium of his alma mater and saw his former teachers and mentors enjoying the game he invented. They were able to witness the fruits of their labor as Morgan presented this new activity for their approval. Morgan's ancestors had built ships, and his own amazing journey brought him to Springfield College to build a new sport. A few detours had led Morgan away from his dream of studying at Cornell and becoming an engineer and had brought him full circle to a school founded on the concept of developing well-rounded people. One can also imagine that over the years, as his new game of volleyball grew in popularity and spread around the world, Morgan must surely have looked back upon this particular day with fond memories.

Morgan Brothers Boatyard
(Courtesy of Buc Williams)

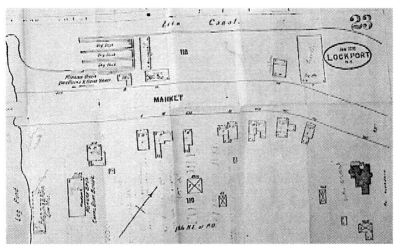

Morgan Brothers Dry Docks and Boatyard Blueprint
(Courtesy of Buc Williams)

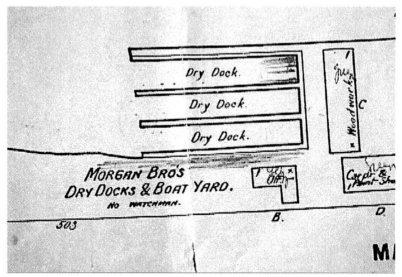

Morgan Brothers Dry Docks and Boatyard Blueprint
(Courtesy of Buc Williams)

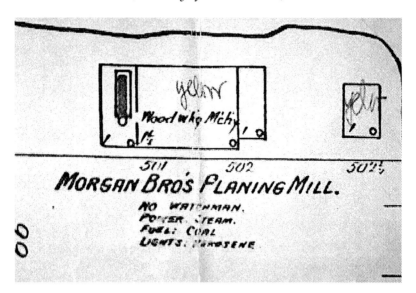

Morgan Brothers Dry Docks and Boatyard Blueprint
(Courtesy of Buc Williams)

Morgan Brothers Boatyard
(Courtesy of Buc Williams)

Morgan Brothers Boatyard
(Courtesy of Buc Williams)

Morgan Brothers Boatyard
(Courtesy of Buc Williams)

Morgan (top right corner) with Mount Hermon Football Team
(Courtesy of Buc Williams)

Morgan (top left corner) and the Springfield College
Football Team, 1893
(Courtesy of the Springfield College Archives)

Morgan (top right corner) with the Springfield College
Class of 1894
(Courtesy of the Springfield College Archives)

Holyoke YMCA — Birthplace of Volleyball
(Courtesy of the Volleyball Hall of Fame)

Holyoke YMCA Interior — Birthplace of Volleyball
(Courtesy of the Volleyball Hall of Fame)

A. G. Spalding
(Courtesy of the Spalding Archives)

Morgan (circled) with "Mintonette" Exhibition Team
(Courtesy of the Volleyball Hall of Fame)

WILLIAM G. MORGAN.
The Inventor of Volley Ball.

Hayes, Photo.

William G. Morgan
(Courtesy of the Spalding Archives)

Morgan (lower right corner) and his family
(Courtesy of Buc Williams)

ERNEST M. BEST, PRESIDENT
HERBERT L. PRATT, VICE-PRESIDENT

WILLIAM M. KINGSLEY, TREASURER
WALLACE V. CAMP, ASSISTANT TREASURER

BENJAMIN A. FRANKLIN
CHAIRMAN EXECUTIVE COMMITTEE

SPRINGFIELD COLLEGE

CORPORATE NAME
INTERNATIONAL YOUNG MEN'S CHRISTIAN ASSOCIATION COLLEGE

SPRINGFIELD, MASSACHUSETTS

COMMITTEE ON ADMISSIONS

March 2, 1938

Memorandum to Miss G. Carr

From   George O Draper

Re: Mr. William G. Morgan, Inventor of Volley Ball

Mr. Morgan was on the Campus yesterday afternoon and I had hoped to have you meet him, but time did not permit. He was quite anxious to have our records complete concerning him.

As the inventor of Volley Ball, he doubtless will go down in history. I got the following information from him which you may want for your records. His father was a Welshman by the name of George Henry Morgan. His mother was Nancy Chatfield of Northfield, Vermont. William George Morgan was born at Lockport, New York on January 23, 1870. He married Mary King Coldwell of West Northfield, Massachusetts. He met her while a student at Mt. Herman. He sang with the quartette and she acted as accompanist.

It was Mr. James Naismith who first interested Morgan in coming to Springfield. Morgan was playing center on the Mt. Herman football team which played a game against Springfield in the city of Pittsfield. Naismith was impressed with young Morgan's playing and invited him to come to Springfield as the football team needed a center. The first real Volley Ball game ever played, according to Mr Morgan was played in our old gymnasium. He brought down two teams and demonstrated the game which he called "Mintinette". Dr. Halsted suggested that Volley Ball would be a better name and Morgan immediately adopted it.

[Mintonette]

OD:m

GV
1017
V6
M5
[no.1:
Rare book room]

Memo from George Draper Following Morgan's 1938
Visit to Springfield College
(Courtesy of the Springfield College Archives)

Banquet Honoring Morgan at Lockport, New York, YMCA, 1939
(Courtesy of the Spalding Archives)

Morgan wearing his "S" sweater
(Courtesy of the Springfield College Archives)

William G. Morgan Volleyball Hall of Fame Induction Photo
(Courtesy of the Volleyball Hall of Fame)

Morgan Gravestone
(Courtesy of Buc Williams)

7

The Rules

Morgan provided an original set of rules for those interested in stretching a net across a gymnasium and trying out his new concept. Those rules first appeared in the July, 1896 publication of the YMCA called "Physical Education".

Volley Ball

During the past winter Mr. W. G. Morgan of Holyoke, Mass. has developed a game in his gymnasium which is called Volley Ball. It was presented at the Physical Director's Conference, and the general impression seemed to be that it would fill a place not filled by any other game. It is to be played indoors, and by those who wish a game not so rough as basket ball and yet one in which the same degree of activity is demanded. The complete report as given to the Conference by W. G. Morgan is as follows:

Volley Ball is a new game which is pre-eminently fitted for the gymnasium or the exercise hall, but which may be played out of doors. Any number of persons may play the game. The play consists of keeping a ball in motion over a high net, from one side to the other, thus partaking of the character of two games—tennis and hand ball.

Play is started by a player on one side serving the ball over the net into the opponents' field or court. The opponents then, without allowing the ball to strike the floor, return it, and it is in this way kept going back and forth until one side fails to return it or it hits the floor. This counts a "score" for one side or a "server out" for the other, depending upon the side in point. The game consists of nine innings, each side serving a certain number of times, as per rules, in each inning.

Rules of Volley Ball

1. GAME. The game consists of nine innings.

2. INNING. An inning consists of: when one person is playing on each side, one service on each side; when two are playing on each side, two services on each side; when three or more are playing on each side, three services on each side. The man serving continues to do so until out by failure of his side to return the ball. Each man shall serve in turn.

3. COURT. The court or floor space shall be twenty-five feet wide and fifty feet long, to be divided into two square courts, twenty-five by twenty-five feet, by the net. Four feet from the net on either side and parallel with it shall be a line across the court, the Dribbling line. The boundary lines must be plainly marked so as to be visible from all parts of the courts. Note.— The exact size of the court may be changed to suit the convenience of the place.

4. NET. The net shall be at least two feet wide and twenty-seven feet long, and shall be suspended from uprights placed at least one foot outside

the side lines. The TOP LINE of the net must be six feet six inches from the floor.

5. BALL. The ball shall be a rubber bladder covered with leather or canvas. It shall measure not less than twenty-five inches nor more than twenty-seven inches in circumference, and shall weigh not less than nine ounces nor more than twelve ounces.

6. SERVER AND SERVICE. The server shall stand with one foot on the back line. The ball must be batted with the hand. Two services or trials are allowed him to place the ball in the opponents' court (as in tennis). The server may serve into the opponents' court at any place. In a service the ball must be batted at least ten feet, no dribbling allowed. A service which would strike the net, but is struck by another of the same side before striking the net, if it goes over into the opponents' court, is good, but if it should go outside, the server has no second trial.

7. SCORING. Each good service unreturned or ball in play unreturned by the side receiving, counts one score for the side serving. A side only scores when serving, as a failure to return the ball on their part results in the server being put out.

8. NET BALL. A ball which hits the net aside from the first service is called a net ball and is equivalent to a failure to return, counting for the opposite side. The ball hitting the net on first service shall be called *dead*, and counts as a trial.

9. LINE BALL. It is a ball striking the boundary line; it is equivalent to one out of court and counts as such.

10. PLAY AND NUMBERS. Any number may

play that is convenient to the place. A player should be able to cover about ten by ten feet.

Should any player during play touch the net, it puts the ball out of play and counts against his side. Should any player catch or hold for an instant the ball, it is out of play and counts for the opposite side. Should the ball strike any object other than the floor and bound back into the court, it is still in play.

To dribble the ball is to carry it all the time keeping it bouncing. When dribbling the ball no player shall cross the Dribbling line, this putting the ball out of play and counting against him.

Any player, except the captain, addressing the umpire or casting any slurring remarks at him or any of the players on the opposite side, may be disqualified and his side may be compelled to play the game without him or substitute or forfeit the same.[1]

Some of Morgan's rules have stood the test of time. Examples would include the initiation of each play with a serve, the net separating the opponents, and the size of the ball. However, in most cases the game was transformed relatively quickly by the adoption of new rules. In America, volleyball grew in part through its introduction into YMCA programs. Tracking the evolution of rule changes to Morgan's original set of rules demonstrates how the game developed.

The game originally comprised nine innings, but by the turn of the century, the scoring was changed to points and innings were eliminated. Twenty-one points were needed to win a game of volleyball, and by 1917, this number was changed to fifteen, which stood for decades.[2] In 1923, the idea of winning by two was initiated with a rule requiring a team to win two points in succession when the score was tied at fourteen, and two years later, this rule was modified to state that at fourteen all, a team must score two more than its opponents to win.[3]

The dimensions of the court changed in 1912, with an enlargement of the space required to thirty-five feet by sixty feet. Additionally, a ceiling clearance of fifteen feet was recommended because the ball was no longer just being batted across the net.[4] New techniques were being used in serving and reception of the ball, causing the ball to be sent much higher in the air than the height of the net. By 1923, a slight change resulted in a thirty by sixty foot court.[5]

Dribbling the ball was originally mentioned in Morgan's rules as it related to the boundary line that was established four feet from the net. By 1900, dribbling was no longer allowed,[6] and by the early 1920s, a centerline was added as an additional boundary line, preventing players from stepping on to any part of the opponent's court.[7]

The net was raised by a foot in 1900, and in 1912, it was required to be three feet in width.[8] By 1917, the net height was established as eight feet from the floor,[9] and this height essentially remained the standard for the men's game into the twenty-first century. In the 2004 Olympic Games in Athens, the men's competition was played with a net that was 2.43 meters (7 feet, 11 5/8 inches) from the floor. By the early 1940s, the recommended height of the net for women's play was seven feet, six inches from the floor, although the rules stated that "it may be lowered even more if the circumstances warrant it."[10] The women's competition at the 2004 Olympics was 2.24 meters (7 feet, 4 1/8 inches) from the floor.

The circumference of the ball has remained the same, although the original rule calling for a ball twenty-five to twenty-seven inches was changed slightly in 1912. The new rule required a ball twenty-seven to twenty-nine inches in circumference,[11] but just five years later, the original rule was reestablished.

Originally, the server stood with one foot on the back line. This rule was changed by 1912 to require servers to stand anywhere behind the back line, or endline, to initiate the service. By 1916, the service area began to be restricted to the back right or left corners of the endline. Throughout much of the

1900s, most participants were required to serve from the right back portion of the endline area. The net serve was declared a fault in 1900. The original concept of a teammate helping the ball over the net may still apply in backyard volleyball settings, but this rule was officially changed in 1917.[12] By the twenty-first century, rule changes borrowed from some of the initial regulations. Servers could now stand anywhere along the endline to serve, and net serves were no longer considered faults, as play continues once the netted serve crosses to the opponent.

For many decades, one aspect of the scoring of Morgan's sport stood the test of time. Teams could only score when they were serving. In 1988, rally scoring was first introduced to the sport. Rally scoring, in which every play produces a point, was used only in the deciding game of a contest. The concept of rally scoring gained momentum throughout the 1990s, and eventually the rally scoring method was implemented for all games of a match. Another unique ingredient of volleyball is the rotation rule. In 1912, the retiring side would rotate once they had lost a rally on their own serve.[13] This rule was adjusted in 1917 to require the team gaining control of the serve to rotate prior to their next turn of service.

Rallies often result in the ball touching the net during play. The net ball was originally treated in the same fashion as the net serve. All net balls were considered a fault. In 1900, net balls during rallies were allowed, and this rule is still followed today.[14]

The potential for boundary-line disputes has increased over time. The ball travels at incredible speeds, and line judges and officials have only a brief glimpse of the ball contacting the floor. Morgan's initial thinking resulted in the decision to consider the line ball out, but by 1900, the rule makers reversed this idea, and from that time forward any ball landing on a part of a boundary line was considered in.[15]

In the original rules, the numbers of players allowed on the court was flexible, but in 1917, the number of players was listed as six per side.[16] The six-person game remains the most commonly utilized format, but the beach doubles format takes full advantage of Morgan's preliminary concept of incorporating options for the number of players on the court at any one time. Original games with large bunches of players only exacerbated the congestion of the playing area. The six-person setup naturally led to the front and back row identification of players and their responsibilities on the court.

Finally, a few other original violations resulted in rule modifications that have impacted some commonly accepted aspects of volleyball. The number of contacts per side was initially unlimited. The three-contact rule, limiting each side to a maximum of three touches before the ball must be sent across the net, is generally attributed to a rule first adopted in the Philippines in 1912.

Elwood S. Brown is credited with introducing the game in the Philippines. His account of the development of the three-contact rule and the introduction of the spike was included in the 1917–18 Official Volley Ball Rules published by the American Sports Publishing Company. Brown provides an interesting summary of the Filipino approach to the sport and their remarkable contribution to its technical advancement.

> I can well remember the first game. After explaining the simple rules in force at that time, the whistle was blown and the game started. The Filipinos seemed starved for play and they batted the ball back and forth with the utmost enthusiasm and abandon. It was some time before it was possible to get them to pay any attention to "side out" or the scoring of points. Two styles of game are played here, the chief point of distinction lying in the number of times the ball may be struck before being batted over the net. As the Americans play it, the ball may be struck any number of times on one side of the net before returning it over the net into the opponent's territory. The rules used by Filipinos read on this point: the ball must be

touched only three times within a court before being returned over the net; in case the ball is driven into the net one additional touch shall be allowed.

The reason for the rule allowing the Americans to strike the ball any number of times on one side of the net and the Filipinos only three times, does not lie in a whim of the rule makers, but it is an exemplification of a fundamental difference in the two races. The American does everything direct—in volleyball each man usually tries to put the ball into the opponents' territory every time he hits the ball. The Filipino does things indirectly, he likes to tease the mouse awhile— in volleyball to pretend that he is about to put it over the net and then not do so.

It must be said that the Filipinos have developed unusual and surprising skill at keeping the ball in the air and controlling its movements without violating the rules which prohibit catching or holding. I once witnessed a championship game where the players of both teams were anxious to demonstrate their skill in handling the ball. Every time it went over the net the players of the receiving side would bat it back and forth among themselves—up to the net as if about to put it over and then back to the rear line and so on indefinitely. When one team struck the ball fifty-two times on its own side of the net without attempting to put it over, the rules committee, the members of which were present decided to make a drastic change, as the game was developing into something as dinkey as Ping-Pong. Hence the rule reducing the number of touches to three. This has produced a fast, skillfully played game, where every player must be alert and careful not to waste a stroke[17].

Brown then goes on to discuss the evolution of the volleyball spike.

> The Filipinos have developed an interesting play called the Bomba or kill. The player who gives the ball the killing swat is called the Bomberino. The Bomberinos usually play in the second line from the net. On the first stroke allowed the player taking it tries to bat the ball to a point in his own court near the net. On the second stroke one of the net men bats the ball straight up, high into the air, so that it will fall very close to the net. On the third and last strike one of the Bomberinos comes in on the run, jumps high into the air, meets the ball as far above the net as he can jump and reach and smashes it down into the opponents' court. Some of these bomberinos can place the ball as accurately as an expert tennis player returns a tennis ball. Great skill has also been developed in receiving and returning "killed" balls, and so the game goes merrily on.[18]

By 1917, the three-contact rule also clarified that no player could contact the ball twice in succession, and that rule remains in place with two exceptions: (1) a blocked ball in the indoor game does not count as an individual or team contact and (2) a double contact is allowed for an individual's contact of a first ball crossing the net, which typically is a serve or an attack.

Today, gymnasiums and large indoor arenas have much higher ceilings than the Holyoke YMCA that employed William Morgan, so his initial allowance of playing a ball that bounced off any object was useful in keeping play going. Currently, players are allowed to play a ball that touches the ceiling on their side of the court, but a ball touching a wall is out of play.

The game continues to reflect rule changes regarding minimum ceiling height requirements. In addition, Morgan did not present his rules without consideration of etiquette.

Slurring remarks toward opponents or officials were frowned upon from the earliest formation of volleyball, and today officials keep yellow and red cards in their pockets to respond to an ever-growing list of specifically itemized behavioral infractions.

8

Post-YMCA Years — Lillian's View

Even as Morgan's game of volleyball was beginning to spread across the country and even to other nations, William was closing in on the end of his YMCA career. He left the Holyoke YMCA for a brief stop at the New Haven, Connecticut, YMCA, and in 1898, he returned to Lockport with Mary and their three children, Lillian, George, and their youngest child, Robert.

Morgan is listed in Lockport YMCA records as the physical director from October of 1898 to January of 1900. He had returned to his roots, back along the banks of the Erie Canal, now in the role of a community leader at the local YMCA. During Morgan's tenure at the Lockport YMCA, a fourth child, James, was born. It appears that the responsibility of a growing family contributed to his decision to leave YMCA work. The Morgan brothers' business was still booming, and while many reports have accurately indicated that William left YMCA work to pursue that once sought-after engineering career, it appears that not all of his plans developed quite as nicely as his invention of volleyball.

William's daughter, Lillian Morgan Hewitt, at the age of eighty-four, prepared and presented a look back at the Morgan family as she remembered it in the early 1900s. Lillian provides some insight into the next ten years.

My father felt the need for a more lucrative means of providing for the growing family. He had never forgotten his first love—engineering and through study became competent enough to secure employment with the General Electric Co. and their power houses in various states during the next eight years.

I remember living in Secaucus and Jersey City, New Jersey, and Quincy, Massachusetts, and life was very comfortable. It was at this point that my father made a most unfortunate decision, he was to regret the rest of his life. He had been working in a power house at Iron Mountain in upstate New York when in one of his travels he met a man from Texas who persuaded him to invest his savings and Mother's inheritance in a lumber business at Port Bolivar, Texas. It was a traumatic move to make and it preyed on my Mother's mind so that she became very ill. We employed a nurse to care for her. Finally, the doctor asked Mother if there was something on her mind troubling her and she confessed she was sure the planned move to Texas was the wrong one. She recovered and we crated our furniture—piano and all—had it loaded on a boat, the *Alamo*: leaving Rhode Island bound for Galveston, Texas.

The trip was exciting. I recall the ship docked at Key West, Florida, for exchange of freight one night and it was interesting looking down over the rail watching the maneuvers below. I believe it was three days before we docked at Galveston Island. It was summer and HOT! While we waited for our furniture to be unloaded and delivered by ferry to Port Bolivar across the bay, we lived a few days at a hotel in Galveston. I recall the boys went in swimming and were painfully sunburned.

Our new home, a four-room bungalow, was surrounded by a fence to keep away the stock roaming the prairie just beyond. The large lumber mill was located along the railroad track—a short distance from the house. We had no conveniences whatever. The Gulf of Mexico was about a half mile beyond the buildings and neighbors were few and far between.

There was a one-room schoolhouse a couple of miles away around the "point." Each morning, Dad would hitch the big sorrel horse—one of two horses belonging to the mill—hitch him up to the "surrey with the fringe on top" and take us to school singing all the way. We would pick up two neighborhood children along the route. There was quite a turnover in teachers in that one-room schoolhouse—pay was little and the school small. One teacher, a lovely redhead fell in love with the young preacher and was married before the year was out. We all watched that romance with interest and regret.

There was a tall lighthouse at Port Bolivar, a short distance from the coast and not far from the mill and our house and the new homes nearby. I shall never forget that fall of 1910. In 1900, there was such a disastrous storm sweep across the Island of Galveston in the Gulf of Mexico and took hundred of lives, that the government erected a high sea wall around the island. That fall of 1910 we lived through a similar storm, but Port Bolivar had no such protection from the violent winds and waves.

During the day the winds and rain had been steadily building up until we decided we should take shelter in a cement building connected with the mill. So, holding hands (no one—alone—could stand against the force of the wind), the family struggled to reach the building. Safely inside we looked out the high windows toward the Gulf of Mexico—its waves getting higher and more fierce. Then word came to us to go to the lighthouse for safety. With help we scaled the fences (like birds) just ahead of the waves which gradually covered all the land up to the foot of the lighthouse. Then a chain was fastened to the lighthouse through the howling winds. After several hours we were told the water was receding.

By morning we were informed we could return to our homes—to clean up the slimy water-soaked rugs, etc. All our chickens were drowned except the ones on the top roost. It was a heartbreaking time for everyone. All the pools and ponds on the prairie had been turned into salt water and we had to pump the salt water from our well before we had fresh water to drink. We weren't able to supply fresh water for all the animals that surrounded our well—and hundreds died on the prairie.

Some weeks later as we stood outdoors we became conscious of a buzzing sound. Looking up we saw a brown sky settling down upon us. In seconds we were completely covered by mosquitoes and running for cover wasn't much help. They were there too. The only solution was to drape netting over each bed, wrap newspapers under our clothing, around our arms and legs and draw stockings over the papers. We wore straw hats covered by netting. It was a help to keep a smudge going night and day in the house by burning damp clothes in a metal container.

During that time my brother Bob developed typhoid and I remember, as the doctor drove up to the house, you couldn't tell the color of the horse—it was completely covered with mosquitoes. I can't remember how long the mosquitoes stayed with us, but they finally left and Bob recovered, with prayer and Mother's excellent care.

About two weeks later we had a second onslaught of mosquitoes and it was then that Dad announced, "We've had it." We packed up our belongings, shipped them by rail with them headed for Lockport and my grandparents home. They had already taken in a daughter and her two sons whose father was a gambler, but what were six more! Their hearts and home were big enough! And I look back on that winter—eleven in the family with a great deal of warmth and happiness. My father soon found work and from then on he never opened his pay envelope, but handed it unopened to Mother—just his way of showing his appreciation and love.[1]

Lillian's family review provides a glimpse of Morgan the family man. His adventurous spirit was most notable first as a young man pursuing an education. His excursion to Texas obviously persuaded him to return to his hometown of Lockport. It's interesting to note that while William G. Morgan and his family were surviving their disaster in Texas in 1910, the Morgan Brothers Boat Building Company was approaching the end of its profitable and historic business. The canal was widened just beyond the Morgan Brothers building, and their dry dock was put out of business.[2]

The Morgans were resilient as a family. William was eventually employed by the Harrison Radiator Corporation in 1920 and worked as a millwright and inspector until his retirement in 1939.

9

Volleyball Across the Globe

The spread of volleyball globally has been well chronicled. While Morgan gets the much-deserved credit for originating the idea, it is likely that he never dreamed his new game would reach the far corners of the earth.

Even as Morgan was traveling in the first ten years of the twentieth century, his game was being introduced in other countries. Volleyball found its way to Canada in 1900 and Cuba in 1905.[1] Hyozo Omori, a 1907 graduate of the International YMCA Training School is credited with introducing the game to Japan the following year while working at the Tokyo YMCA,[2] and by 1910, reports circulated of volleyball games being played in the Philippines.[3]

In 1912, at the same time the three-contact rule was first used in the Philippines, the first United States Open of Volleyball took place. The game gained great popularity in YMCAs, and this international organization assisted in the arrival of volleyball in Uruguay, England, and Brazil in 1912, 1914, and 1917, respectively.[4]

It is often noted that sixteen thousand volleyballs were distributed by expeditionary forces to U.S. troops and allied forces in 1915, yet another contributing factor in the international growth of volleyball. Elwood Brown was highly involved in the global development of the game, moving on from the Philippines to establish the Far Eastern Games and actually drew up the initial plans for the Inter-Allied Games that eventually were established in Europe following World War I.[5]

Even as volleyball grew as a competitive sport, Morgan's initial desire to provide a game for businessmen to play appears to have prospered in it's own development. E. W. Roehm of Columbus, Ohio provided a look at the growth of volleyball for businessmen in the 1917 Official Rules Book.

> For some twenty years the writer has had the privilege of including the game of volley ball in his gymnasium schedules. It has been a winner ever since and proves to be a game enjoyable and decidedly profitable for men of all ages and classes. In the introduction of the game in the four different fields of my labors, it had to directly compete for place with basketball which game when taken seriously by men in middle life was entirely too severe. Volley ball continued to grow into favor and now stands out pre-eminently as the best all around game for men ever invented.[6]

These comments provide quite an endorsement for Morgan and his game. Volleyball was standing the test of time. Roehm goes on to point out that "volley ball is well suited for men, balancing work and rest into a splendid active and relaxing blending". While Roehm compares the popularity of volleyball to basketball, R. C. Cubbon, who was serving as the Physical Director at the Providence, RI YMCA, takes it a step further in the same 1917 edition of the Official Volleyball Rules. In his article, "A New National Game", he suggests that volleyball is ready to rival baseball as the national pastime.

> During the past few years a new game has appeared on the athletic horizon and its popularity has so increased that today it is

demanding recognition as one of our national games—this game of volley ball. The casual observer or newspaper athlete would probably at once relegate it to second place with base ball, foot ball and basket ball as its superiors, but interest has been developing so rapidly that it has a right to challenge for first place.[7]

Considering the fact that Morgan also wrote an article that was published in this same edition of the 1917 Official Rules, it is more than likely that he read Cubbon's comments. Morgan most assuredly was able to observe the rapid growth of his game, and must have found it's rapid rise very satisfying. Cubbon goes on to point out that

It is a recognized fact that base ball is the national game at the present time, but during the past two decades certain restrictions have been growing about this great game which are bound sooner or later to relegate it to a certain more limited group. I refer to the rapid development of congested city life which has increased property values to the extent that city land for base ball is held at prohibitive prices. Base ball today has surrendered to the suburban towns, the rural districts, our educational institutions and professionalism. Base ball requires 4000 square feet and foot ball 1500 square feet per player. These conditions will sooner or later jeopardize the popularity of the game. If this is true and if we are becoming a game-loving people, and since we need games for our health's sake, we must look for additional sports.[8]

Cubbon attended Springfield College and is listed as a student in 1909, just fifteen years after Morgan graduated. He trumpeted the growth of volleyball beyond his call for it's consideration as our new national game. He is credited with organizing the first National YMCA tournament, held at

Brooklyn College in 1922[9] and he "was one of the first to urge his fellow volleyball enthusiasts to have volleyball included in the Olympic Games".[10]

In the United States, as the game continued to develop through YMCA regional and national competitions, intercollegiate and interscholastic competition was also growing. High school volleyball was on the scene by 1917[11], and by 1924 boys and girls varsity volleyball teams had been formed in the Pittsburgh, Pennsylvania area.[12] The introduction of volleyball at the collegiate level was also apparent during this time period as reports circulated in 1928 of a collegiate conference being formed in Oregon.[13]

By this time, William Morgan was working in what would be his final job, as an inspector for Harrison Radiator in Lockport. Morgan was surely hearing reports of the continuing growth of the game. By 1928, the Soviet Union, just three years after forming their own set of volleyball rules, held national championships for both women's and men's divisions. This was the same year that the United States Volleyball Association was formed primarily "to publish the rules, promote tournaments and to unite all organizations interested in the promotion of the game and to represent the interests of volleyball internationally."[14]

In 1928, Katherine Montgomery authored the first textbook on volleyball, *Volleyball for Women*. Many published reviews of the history of volleyball indicate that Robert Laveaga's 1933 book, *Volleyball—A Man's Game*, was the first book published. Perhaps the title of his book is better understood as a reaction to a more accurate account rightfully crediting Montgomery with her publication. In fact, the preface of Laveaga's book addresses this as follows, "Miss Alice W. Frymier, of A. S. Barnes and Company, Inc., kindly and thoughtfully suggested the name for this book, namely, *Volley Ball—A Man's Game*. This suggestion was given in view of the fact that there is a book on the market with the title of *Volley Ball* which is written for women".[15]

Throughout the 1930s and 1940s, volleyball in the United States grew in popularity and appears to have been often more popular as a girl's sport than a readily accepted option for boys.

However, opportunities were limited for the administration of and support of girls athletic programs throughout this time and beyond. At the College level the game continued to move forward. The University of Washington became the first in 1934 to play in an open tournament,[16] and in 1935, approximately 700 cities reported over 175,000 participants in recreation programs.[17]

Morgan surely was aware of the many dedicated ambassadors of the game, and it is interesting to note that many had Springfield College connections. George Fisher received an honorary degree from Springfield College in 1909.[18] He was the long time editor of volleyball rules, USVBA President and was even referred to as the "father of volleyball".[19] Harry A. Batchelor graduated from Springfield College in 1917. His teams won the first five National YMCA Championships, and was often referred to as a "coach of coaches".[20] Robert Laveaga wrote a second book, *Volley Ball* in 1942 (dedicated to George Fisher) and he completed his illustrious career as a Professor at Springfield College from 1953 to 1957.[21]

The Federation Internationale de Volleyball was formed in Paris in 1947, and by 1949, the first ever World Championships took place in Prague. By this time, Harold Friermood, who was the national director of health and physical education for the National Board of the YMCA from 1943 to 1968, had already begun his campaign for the inclusion of volleyball as an Olympic sport. Friermood also served as president of the United States Volleyball Association (USVBA) from 1952 to 1955 and vice president of the Federation Internationale de Volleyball (FIVB) from 1951 to 1960. In 1964, at the Tokyo Olympics, Friermood witnessed the realization of his dream, and Morgan's game was again honored with distinction as it was formally accepted as an Olympic sport.

Volleyball, though an American invention, received most of its modern-day technical and tactical development from many international sources. The Tokyo Olympics perhaps signified the greatest exposure of a newer, faster competitive sport, in large part due to two Japanese coaches. Yatutaka Matsudaira was the coach of the Japanese men's team, and he promoted their quick system of offensive attacks using multiple options and a variety of tempos. His team won the bronze medal at the 1964 Olympic Games, the silver in Mexico City four years later, and a gold medal in the 1972 Munich games.

At the same time, the Japanese women's volleyball team received worldwide fame for their relentless defense, most notably the rolling dive technique drilled into them by Hirofumi Daimatsu, who became known as the "demon coach." The intensity with which he trained his women's team is credited with revolutionizing attitudes toward training female athletes. High-intensity conditioning and strict discipline were the hallmarks of his coaching approach to elite women players. The game of volleyball from that point on, when played at its highest levels, combined a great blend of power and speed.

In some ways, the development of the game came full circle in 1984, as the USA men's volleyball team, led by head coach Doug Beal, captured the gold medal in Los Angeles. Coach Beal, along with assistant coach Bill Neville, is credited with an innovative offensive system built around one of the game's all-time greats, Karch Kiraly. In the USA system, only two players were responsible for covering the entire court and receiving the serve on every offensive rotation. This specialized concept combined with new attack approach patterns and defensive blocking systems revolutionized the way the game was played.

Rules related to specialization continue to be implemented today. In 1998, the FIVB announced the adoption of the "libero player." A libero, designated by a contrasting colored uniform, is allowed unlimited substitutions for back-row players and is limited by rule from participating in attacking and blocking.

By the turn of the twenty-first century, the modern game of volleyball bore little resemblance to the initial game of mintonette that William G. Morgan developed back at the Holyoke YMCA. The transformation of the game, however, has been in keeping with Morgan's vision for an enjoyable activity. Volleyball is fun to play and observe. The game continues to gain popularity worldwide, both in participation levels and as an entertainment vehicle for fans.

10

Morgan and His Game Honored

On March 1, 1938, William G. Morgan returned to Springfield College for the first time in forty-two years. Although his brief visit caught the campus administrators and faculty by surprise, he was quickly and warmly welcomed. Morgan returned to the school's gymnasium, where his first exhibition game had been played. At the time of that exhibition, the East Gymnasium was the only completed building on the grounds. The West Gymnasium had since been added to the building, along with other new facilities on campus including a dorm, a library, and a dining hall.

Morgan was impressed by the development of the campus. He arrived in Springfield following stops in Pittsburgh, Pennsylvania, and Greenwich, Connecticut, where he took part in volleyball clinics. During his visit to his alma mater, Morgan toured the campus with Professor Leslie J. Judd, a pioneer in the gymnastics field and coach of the Springfield gym team. Morgan was invited to speak to one of the activity classes.

Movies were taken of his impromptu presentation, during which he discussed the circumstances surrounding his invention of volleyball. He wanted the college to have accurate historical records concerning how his game was developed. His visit confirmed many of the details already published regarding the exhibition game in 1896.

The March 1938 Springfield College Bulletin notes that "during his visit Mr. Morgan pointed out that he never intended that volleyball should become a competitive sport or compete with basketball for popularity. The chief purposes for the game have always been exercise and enjoyment".[1]

On March 22, 1939, Morgan was honored in his hometown of Lockport by representatives of Springfield College, including the men's gymnastics team. A banquet took place at the Lockport YMCA, and legendary Springfield College gymnastics coach Leslie J. Judd presented Morgan with the Springfield Block S sweater in recognition of his alumni status and his contribution to the world of sport. Judd's gymnastics exhibition teams had by this time gained great notoriety from worldwide travels and performances. The team performed in the Lockport YMCA auditorium following the banquet. As reported in the March 23 edition of the *Lockport Union-Sun & Journal*, "a capacity audience watched a thrilling demonstration of gymnastic art staged by the college gym team. Exercises on the rings, side bars, parallel bars, long horse and spring board were capped by exhibitions of group saber, wand and Indian club drills. The performance was brought to a close by a series of tableaux in which the men, covered with a silver preparation, formed human sculpture groups."[2]

Morgan's comments at this event included his reflections on the growth and development of his sport. As reported in the same *Union-Sun & Journal* article, Morgan said he "invented the game for men of middle age who found basketball too strenuous. Volleyball was not intended to replace basketball as a competitive sport. I saw a need for a game for older men which would not require the stamina or close physical checking called for by basketball. In that respect I feel that it has succeeded, and I am glad that the game has found a place in gymnasiums all over the world."[3]

Just a few short years later, on December 27, 1942, William G. Morgan died following a long illness. Funeral services took place at his home in Lockport on Monday, December 28. The *Lockport Union-Sun & Journal* reported that "a few days before his death Mr. Morgan received a copy of the 1943 volleyball rule book published by the U.S. Volleyball Association and a testimonial letter from Dr. George J. Fisher, its president, in which Dr. Fisher pointed out that widespread use by the armed forces has taken the game to far-distant points. Those of us who appreciate this game and have promoted it over the years are conscious of our indebtedness to you. Your name will be permanently linked to the game as long as it continues."[4]

In 1951, Springfield College served as the host for the USVBA Men's National Championship. As part of this event, the USVBA honored Morgan for his contribution to the sport. R. George Morgan, eldest son of the game's originator, accepted an invitation from Dr. George Fisher, the USVBA president, and Springfield College Volleyball Coach, M. L. "Doc" Walters, the executive secretary of the tournament, to represent the Morgan family. He received a special citation and a memorial plaque signed by Fisher and Harold Friermood honoring his father for his contributions to athletics and recreation.

The plaque reads as follows:

> It is fitting that the annual meeting of the USVBA should be held on the campus of Springfield College for here was the birthplace of basketball, and here also four years later in 1895 a new game evolved from the former, was demonstrated. Thus in Springfield College two informal games, world-wide in their acceptance, were created which greatly enriched the recreational opportunities of countless people in many nations. To William G. Morgan, founder of volleyball while Physical Director at Holyoke Y and to the College which inspired him, the USVBA extends high tribute in appreciation of his notable and generous contributions.[5]

On May 9, 1955, R. George Morgan represented his father and family at a Recognition Dinner held at the Lockport YMCA. Don Meyncke, the Branch Executive of the Buffalo YMCA presented a review of the life of William G. Morgan and awarded his son the Helms Athletic Foundation Volleyball Hall of Fame plaque posthumously.[6]

The Volleyball Hall of Fame in Holyoke, Massachusetts, was first incorporated in 1978. The roots for the establishment of this local shrine can be traced back to 1971. USVBA board member John O'Donnell and USVBA region one chairman of officials, Peter Meltzer, spearheaded efforts to promote the seventy-fifth anniversary of the sport. As Holyoke residents and members of the city's Chamber of Commerce, both men worked along with the Chambers Chargers Committee, promoting Holyoke as the "birthplace of volleyball." The first Morgan Memorial Tournament was played in 1971, and this long-running event helped bring attention to the city of Holyoke and to their noteworthy history in sport. The USVBA designated the Holyoke Public Library as a repository for volleyball memorabilia. Primarily through the efforts of a largely volunteer base of local men and women serving on the board of directors, the Hall of Fame initiated its first induction ceremony in 1985, honoring William G. Morgan as the first and only inductee in their inaugural class.

In addition to honoring inductees in the categories of players, coaches, officials, and leaders, the Volleyball Hall of Fame created the William G. Morgan Award in 1994 to recognize companies and organizations who have contributed significantly to the promotion of the sport.

The centennial celebration of volleyball in 1995 produced even more posthumous awards for Morgan. Mary Morgan Quackenbush, granddaughter of William G. Morgan, established the William G. Morgan Foundation in 1989. In 1995, Edward V. Crowe served as president of this organization as they sponsored a three-day festival in Lockport to honor their native son. According to *The Buffalo News*, events scheduled for July 28 through 30 were held to commemorate Morgan's achievement. Four sand volleyball courts and a granite monument bearing Morgan's name were dedicated in the community's Outwater Park.[7]

When asked to reflect on her grandfather and the significance of this event, Quackenbush said, "I'm sure he knows he's being recognized, but if he were alive he would be embarrassed. He was a quiet man who liked to go down in the coal cellar and smoke his pipe. He had an old easy chair and his pipes down there, and that's where he found peace and quiet. As a little girl, I lived next door to my grandfather in Lockport, and he never talked about volleyball, but now I wish that I'd asked him about it. It's a little late now, but with a lot of people's help, I think we've honored him."[8]

Ed Crowe was pleased with the results of the celebration, and he offered his response in *The Buffalo News*: "It took one hundred years, but it was worth waiting for."[9] Crowe continued his own involvement in researching and promoting Morgan's role in inventing volleyball right up until his death in 1996. With the help of Lockport area photographer Buc Williams, Crowe produced a thirty-minute video, "The William G. Morgan Story," providing most of the narrative himself. Williams completed the project after Crowe's passing.

The Volleyball Hall of Fame in Holyoke created an ambitious schedule of local activities in 1995 to honor the one hundredth year of Morgan's internationally acclaimed game. Events included cohosting the NCAA Men's Championship with Springfield College in May at the Springfield Civic Center. They also hosted the 1995 USVBA National Championships, staging them at nearby Westover Air Force Base in Chicopee, Massachusetts, and completed the year by working with the University of Massachusetts Amherst campus in hosting the NCAA Women's National Championships, which took place in conjunction with the American Volleyball Coaches Convention in Springfield, Massachusetts.

Springfield College recognized the one hundredth year of volleyball at its commencement exercises in 1995 by conferring an honorary degree to Doug Beal, 1984 Coach of the gold-medal winning USA men's team, for his many contributions to the sport of volleyball, invented by their very own William G. Morgan.

Springfield College was honored by the Volleyball Hall of Fame in 1996 with the Court of Honor Award for its significant contributions and commitment to the sport of volleyball. In its proclamation, the Volleyball Hall of Fame announced that no other college or university has had a longer history and greater impact on volleyball than Springfield College.

Both in Lockport, New York, and in the Holyoke area, where he invented the game, Morgan was honored for his crowning achievement as volleyball celebrated its one hundredth birthday.

Recognition of Morgan and those associated with him continues today, as the Lockport YMCA announced in 2006 that Morgan's nephew, Jack Deeringer, left a gift in his estate to the local YMCA. This gift of $150,000, left in honor of his uncle, was allocated to the YMCA's effort to build a new facility.

Perhaps one of the finest tributes to Morgan was written by Erie Chapman, general secretary (1941–1945) of the Lockport YMCA. Mr. Chapman knew William Morgan only during the last few years of Morgan's life and indicated that during their conversations Morgan "was always interested in learning of any new developments in the game."[10] He goes on to share that "the world of sport has lost a true friend and we shall always be indebted to this kindly gentleman who provided health and happiness of millions by the invention of the game of volleyball."[11] Chapman includes the following thoughts in his summary of Morgan's crowning achievement:

> It is only the privilege of the few to leave behind to posterity something which will enrich the lives of millions for coming generations. Such was the gift of the late William G. Morgan, the inventor of the game of volleyball, a game which is played around the world by probably more different people and different age ranges than any other game. Rich indeed is the heritage of a bequest such as this to his fellow man and happy and contented was William G. Morgan in making it possible for young and old alike to enjoy the benefits of this fascinating game. The world cannot help being a better world and the people who know and play the game

of volleyball cannot help but be richer in health
and friends because of it.[12]

Morgan's game lives on, played by elite athletes under
bright lights and by friends in backyards against the backdrop
of blue skies. Morgan's idea, his game, is a gift to us all.

About the Author

Joel Dearing is an associate professor of physical education and the head women's volleyball coach at Springfield College in Springfield, Massachusetts. His collegiate teams (both women's and men's) have won more than 800 matches over a span of 36 seasons. He served as the Distinguished Professor of Humanics at Springfield College in 1997-98, and was recognized in 2006 by USA Volleyball, the American Volleyball Coaches Association, and Molten USA with the Trailblazer Award for his role in establishing the Men's Invitational Volleyball Division III Championship a decade earlier. He is currently on the Honorary Board of Directors at the Volleyball Hall of Fame in nearby Holyoke, having served on the Board since 1990. He is the author of *Volleyball Fundamentals*, serves on the USAV CAP CADRE, and directs his own volleyball summer camp. Joel and his wife, Diane, have three children and live in Wilbraham, Massachusetts.

Notes

Introduction
1. The telling of this story led me to discover a long list of Springfield College alumni, faculty, and coaches who contributed to the development of volleyball. Many of these individuals are identified in this book. At least a few more deserve to be mentioned here. Springfield College graduates William Baird (class of 1950) and Wilbur Peck (class of 1952), served as president of the USVBA, and both were inducted into the Volleyball Hall of Fame in the "leader" category (Baird in 1997, Peck in 1999). Bill Odeneal received his first degree from Springfield College in 1949 and had a long and successful collegiate coaching career. His 1968 dissertation, "The History and Contributions of the United States Volleyball Association," proved to be a significant resource as I researched this book, as it has been for countless others who have written about the history of volleyball.

Chapter 1: The Morgans of Lockport, New York
1. Hewitt, "The Morgan Family."
2. Ibid.
3. Ibid.
4. Lewis, "History of Lockport."
5. Farley, "Morgan Boats the Best Around."

Chapter 2: Young Will — "Well Worth Polishing"
1. "Alumnus Who Originated Volleyball Returns to Campus for First Time in 42 Years," Springfield College Archives (1938 Bulletin), p. 11.
2. Northfield Mount Hermon School Archives.
3. Morgan, William G. Admissions application, Northfield Mount Hermon School Archives.
4. Northfield Mount Hermon School Archives.
5. Ibid.
6. Ibid.
7. Ibid.

8. Ibid.
9. Ibid.

Chapter 3: Mount Hermon School — "Lazy Boys Are Not Desired"

1. Gundry, *Love Them In*, p.5.
2. Moody, *The Life of D. L. Moody By His Son*, p. 327.
3. Ibid.
4. *Mount Hermon School Catalog*, 1891–92, Northfield Mount Hermon School Archives.
5. Hewitt, "The Morgan Family."
6. Northfield Mount Hermon School Archives, *The Hermonite*, November 28, 1891.
7. Northfield Mount Hermon School Archives, *The Hermonite*, March 5, 1892.
8. Northfield Mount Hermon School Archives.

Chapter 4: Naismith — The Recruiter

1. Doggett, *Man and a School*, p. 68.
2. Ibid, p. 16.
3. Ibid, pp.67–70.
4. *Eighth Catalogue of the International Young Men's Christian Association Training School*, p. 11. Springfield College Archives.
5. Northfield Mount Hermon School Archives.
6. Northfield Mount Hermon School Archives, *The Hermonite*, November 12, 1892.
7. Training School Notes, p. 74, Springfield College Archives.
8. Ibid, pp. 73–74.
9. *Lockport Union-Sun & Journal*, "Inventor of Volleyball Dies at 72." December 28, 1942.

Chapter 5: Springfield Days

1. *First Statement of the School for Christian Workers*, n. p., Springfield College Archives.
2. Ibid.
3. *Second Statement of the School for Christian Workers*, p.19.
4. Ibid.
5. Ibid, p. 20.

6. Ibid.
7. Ibid.
8. Doggett, p. 43.
9. Moody, *The Life of D. L. Moody By His Son*, p. 339.
10. Gundry, p. 53.
11. Doggett, pp. 53–54.
12. *Eighth Catalogue of the International Young Men's Christian Association Training School*, pp. 7–11, Springfield College Archives.
13. Ibid.
14. *1894 Yearbook*, Springfield College Archives.
15. *1895–96 International YMCA Training School Physical Department Circular*, Springfield College Archives.

Chapter 6: Invention and Exhibition: From Mintonette to Volley Ball

1. Cameron, "The Origin of Volleyball," p. 7.
2. Morgan, "How Volleyball Was Originated," p. 9.
3. Ibid.
4. Allen and Gulick, *Minton*, pp. 3–5.
5. Ibid, pp. 7–8.
6. Mizutani, *Volleyball Its Origin and Development*, pp. 49–53.
7. Chapman, "Life of William G. Morgan." p. 16
8. Morgan, p. 11.
9. Doggett, p. 74.

Chapter 7: The Rules

1. *Physical Education*, pp. 50–51.
2. Laveaga, *Volley Ball – A Man's Game*, pp. 5–8.
3. Ibid, pp.12–13.
4. Ibid, p. 6.
5. Ibid, p. 12.
6. Ibid, p. 6.
7. Ibid, p. 9.
8. Ibid, pp. 5–6.
9. Ibid, p. 6.
10. Laveaga, *Volleyball*, p. 94.
11. Laveaga, *Volleyball – A Man's Game*, p. 6.

12. Ibid, pp. 5–8.
13. Ibid, p. 7.
14. Ibid, p. 5.
15. Ibid.
16. Ibid, p. 8.
17. Brown, "Volley Ball in the Philippines," pp. 87–88.
18. Ibid, pp. 88–89.

Chapter 8: Post-YMCA Years—Lillian's View
1. Hewitt, "The Morgan Family."
2. Farley, "Morgan Boats the Best Around."

Chapter 9: Volleyball Across the Globe
1. Dhanaraj, *Volleyball For Men and Women*, p. 4.
2. Mizutani, *Ball Sports: Basketball and Volleyball*, p. 75.
3. deCastro, *A History of Volleyball in the Philippines*, p. 23.
4. Plotnicki, "A Brief History of Volleyball," p. 28.
5. Odeneal, "The History and Contributions of the United States Volleyball Association." p. 33.
6. Roehm, "Business Men and Volley Ball," p. 37.
7. Cubbon, "A New National Game," p. 29.
8. Ibid, p. 29.
9. Odeneal, p. 52.
10, Ibid, p. 53.
11. Ibid, p. 90.
12. Cole, "The History and Development of Volleyball," p. 9.
13. Odeneal, p. 81.
14. Ibid, p. 3.
15. Laveaga, *Volley Ball—A Man's Game*, p. ix.
16. Odeneal, p. 81.
17. Ibid, p. 83.
18. Ibid, p. 54.
19. Ibid, p. 57.
20. Ibid, pp. 51–52.
21. Ibid, p. 124.

Chapter 10: Morgan and His Game Honored
1."Alumnus Who Originated Volleyball Returns to Campus

for First Time in 42 Years," Springfield College Archives (March, 1938 Bulletin).

2. *Lockport Union-Sun & Journal*, "Volleyball Inventor Receives Letter." March 23, 1939.

3. Ibid.

4. *Lockport Union-Sun & Journal*, "Inventor of Volleyball Dies at 72." December 28, 1942.

5. Odeneal, p. 24.

6. Meyncke, Don H. (typewritten document).

7. Michel, "Inventor of Volleyball is Honored—Lockport Native Credited in Game's Birth 100 Years Ago."

8. Ibid.

9. Ibid.

10. Chapman, "Life of William G. Morgan," (typewritten document).

11. Chapman, "Life of William G. Morgan," p. 15.

12. Ibid, p. 16.

Bibliography

1894 Yearbook. Springfield College Archives.

1895–96 International YMCA Training School Physical Department Circular. Springfield College Archives. Springfield, MA: Clark W. Bryan Co. Printers, 1896.

Allen, W. E. and Gulick, L. *Minton.* Springfield, Massachusetts: The Triangle Publishing Co., 1896.

"Alumnus Who Originated Volleyball Returns to Campus for First Time in 42 years." March 1938 Bulletin, Springfield College Archives.

Annual Official Rules and Reference Guide of the United States Volleyball Association. Berne, IN: USVBA Printers, 1973.

Arsenian, Seth, ed. *The Humanics Philosophy of Springfield College.* Springfield, MA: Springfield College, 1969.

Berthiaume, S. M. "Volley Ball in the State of Washington." *1917–18 Official Volley Ball Rules.* New York: American Sports Publishing Co., 1917.

Brown, Elwood S. "Volley Ball in the Philippine Islands." *1917–18 Official Volley Ball Rules.* New York: American Sports Publishing Co., 1917.

Cameron, J. Y. "The Origin of Volley Ball." *1917–18 Official Volley Ball Rules.* New York: American Sports Publishing Co., 1917.

Chapman, Erie D. "Life of William G. Morgan, The Inventor of Volleyball." Typewritten document from Henry W. Schmidt.

Chapman, Erie D. "Life of William G. Morgan, The Inventor

of Volleyball." *1944 Official United States Volley Ball Association Volley Ball Guide.* New York: A. S. Barnes and Company, 1944.

Cole, Diana L. "The History and Development of Women's Volleyball: 1895 to 1964." Research paper, University of South Dakota, 1992.

Crowe, Ed, and Buc Williams (producers). *The William G. Morgan Story* (video) Sanborn, NY: Rissa Productions.

Cubbon, R. C. "A New National Game." *1917–18 Official Volley Ball Rules.* New York: American Sports Publishing Co., 1917.

deCastro, Jose S. "A History of Volleyball in the Philippines." Master's project, Springfield College, 1954.

Dhanaraj, V. Hubert. *Volleyball For Men and Women.* 6th ed. Calcutta, India: YMCA Publishing House, 1963.

Doggett, Lawrence L. *Man and a School.* New York: Association Press, 1943.

Draper, George O. "William G. Morgan — Inventor of Volley Ball." *1940 Official Volley Ball Rules.* New York: American Sports Publishing Co., 1939.

Eighth Catalogue of the International Young Men's Christian Association Training School. Springfield College Archives. Springfield, MA: Clark W. Bryan Co. Printers, 1893.

Farley, Doug. "Morgan Boats the Best Around." *Lockport Union-Sun & Journal,* December 8, 2006.

First Statement of the School for Christian Workers. Springfield College Archives. Springfield, MA: Louis H. Orr & Co., 1885.

Fisher, George J., ed. *1917–18 Official Volley Ball Rules.* New York: American Sports Publishing Co., 1917.

Gundry, Stanley N. *Love Them In.* 2nd ed. Chicago: Moody Press, 1999.

Hall, L. K. *Doggett of Springfield.* Springfield, MA: Springfield College, 1964.

Hewitt, Lillian M. "The Morgan Family." Prepared and presented by William G. Morgan's granddaughter for the October 25, 1978, meeting of the Elberta Mother's Club.

"Inventor of Volleyball Dies at 72." *Lockport Union-Sun & Journal,* December 28, 1942.

Laveaga, Robert E. *Volley Ball — A Man's Game.* New York: A. S. Barnes and Company, 1933.

Laveaga, Robert E. *Volley Ball.* New York: A. S. Barnes & Co., 1942.

Lewis, Clarence O. "History of Lockport." Pamphlet from the Lockport Historical Society, 1964.

Meyncke, Don H. Remarks from the Helms Athletic Foundation Volleyball Hall of Fame Awards Dinner honoring William G. Morgan. Lockport, NY: 1955.

Michel, L. "Inventor of Volleyball Is Honored — Lockport Native Credited in Game's Birth 100 Years Ago." *The Buffalo News,* July 29, 1995.

Mizutani, Y. *Ball Sports: Basketball and Volleyball.* Tokyo: Iwasaki Shoten Publishers, 1990.

Mizutani, Y. *Volleyball Its Origin and Development.* Tokyo: Heibon-Sha, 1995.

Montgomery, Katherine W. *Volley Ball for Women.* New York: A. S. Barnes & Company, 1928.

Moody, W. R. *The Life of D. L. Moody By His Son.* New York: Fleming H. Revell Company, 1900.

Morgan, William G. Admissions application. Student #1061MH. See Northfield Mount Hermon School Archives, student files, Morgan, William G.

Morgan, William G. "How Volley Ball Was Originated." *1917–18 Official Volleyball Rules.* New York: American Sports Publishing Co., 1917.

Morse, Oliver C., ed. "International Association Training School Notes." Vol. 1, no. 6. Springfield, MA: October 1892.

Ninth Catalogue of the International Young Men's Christian Association Training School. Springfield College Archives. Springfield, MA: Loring & Axtell Printers, 1894.

Northfield Mount Hermon School Archives. *The Hermonite,* November 28, 1891.

Northfield Mount Hermon School Archives. *The Hermonite,* March 5, 1892.

Northfield Mount Hermon School Archives. *The Hermonite,* November 12, 1892.

Northfield Mount Hermon School Archives. *Mount Hermon School Catalog* 1891–92.

Odeneal, William T. "The History and Contributions of the United States Volleyball Association." PhD dissertation, Springfield College, 1968.

Physical Education. Vol. 5, no. 5. Springfield, MA: The Triangle Publishing Co., July 1896.

Plotnicki, Dr. Ben A. "A Brief History of Volleyball." *The 1965 Annual Official Rules and Reference Guide of the United States Volleyball Association.* Berne, IN: USVBA Printers, 1965.

Roehm, E. W. "Business Men and Volley Ball." *1917–18 Official Volleyball Rules.* New York: American Sports Publishing Co., 1917.

Second Statement of the School for Christian Workers. Springfield College Archives. Springfield, MA: Louis H. Orr & Co., 1885.

Seventh Catalogue of the International Young Men's Christian Association Training School. Springfield College Archives. Springfield, MA: Clark W. Bryan Co. Printers, 1892.

Sixth Catalogue of the International Young Men's Christian Association Training School. Springfield College Archives. Springfield, MA: Springfield Printing and Binding Co., 1891.

Straubel, Mark D. "A Historical Review of the Young Men's Christian Association and its role in the Development and Promotion of Volleyball." Unpublished thesis. Springfield College, 1995.

"The Original Game of Volley Ball."(Spalding Archives) *1917–1918 Official Volleyball Rules.* New York: American Sports Publishing Co., 1917.

"Volleyball Inventor Receives 'Letter'." *Lockport Union-Sun & Journal*, March 23, 1939.

Index

Printed in the United States
126089LV00002B/16/A